A _ ...REWELL TO TRUTH

A Farewell to T R U T H

GIANNI VATTIMO

Translated by WILLIAM McCUAIG

Foreword by ROBERT T. VALGENTI

Columbia University Press NEW YORK

COLUMBIA UNIVERSITY PRESS
Publishers Since 1893
NEW YORK   CHICHESTER, WEST SUSSEX

Originally published in Italian as *Addio alla verità*, copyright © 2009 Meltemi Editore
Translation copyright © 2011 Columbia University Press

Library of Congress Cataloging-in-Publication Data
Vattimo, Gianni, 1936–
    [Addio alla verità. English]
    A farewell to truth / Gianni Vattimo ; foreword by Robert T. Valgenti ;
translated by William McCuaig.
        p.   cm.
Includes bibliographical references (p.   ).
ISBN 978-0-231-15308-9 (cloth : alk. paper)—ISBN 978-0-231-52755-2 (e-book)
1. Truth.   I. Title.
B3654.V383A3313 2011
195—dc22

                                                                    2010032008

Columbia University Press books are printed on permanent
and durable acid-free paper.
This book is printed on paper with recycled content.
Printed in the United States of America

c   10 9 8 7 6 5 4 3 2

CONTENTS

GIANNI VATTIMO IS one of those rare thinkers in whom thought and action suffer little separation. From his early political activism to his two terms as a member of the European Parliament, he has transformed nihilism into a vocation on behalf of the causes of democracy, cultural pluralism, and human solidarity. For philosophers and politicians alike, however, the title *Farewell to Truth* risks sounding more like a punch line than a manifesto for political liberation. While the fear might be that such a pronouncement could be mistaken for the expediency of political lies, the more disturbing reality is that all too often in the age of sound bites, twenty-four-hour news cycles, and dwindling attention spans, the invocation of absolutes—religious, natural, economic— has emerged as a common and effective call to arms in the face of an increasingly pluralistic, global society. Paradoxically, the bearers of these absolutes do not simply reject the common idiom of interpretation that Vattimo indicates elsewhere[1] as symptomatic of postmodern Western culture; rather, they are strangely enabled and nourished by it. Having accepted on principle the reality of a relativistic world where there seem to be no facts, only interpretations, they extol the practicality and utility of direct action in the service of an absolute. In such a climate, Vattimo's farewell to truth is not a woeful resignation but a timely call to extinguish the final flashes of metaphysics and resist the belief that only absolute action and sovereign decision can guarantee peaceful coexistence.

Farewell to Truth is not a flat-out rejection of truth per se but the recognition that truth is something we construct. It is therefore not a descriptive claim about the world as it "really is," but in a manner similar to Nietzsche's announcement that "God is dead," the farewell to truth is an interpretation that marks "the commencement, and the very basis, of democracy" (xxxiv) as an epochal truth that is "constructed with consensus and respect for the liberty of everyone" (xxxvi). Democracy is not a truth that must be grounded or deduced but is instead a historical inheritance and political reality to which one must respond, either dogmatically or pluralistically. As a hermeneutic thinker and politician, the challenge for Vattimo has been to articulate a call for human liberation that accepts the interpretative character of truth while not taking its own position as absolute. The validity of Vattimo's position is often criticized as an irresolvable dilemma: either his philosophical commitments are politically expedient and thus merely rationalizations of leftist ideology, or those same commitments are based on a descriptive, and hence unavoidably metaphysical, claim about reality.[2] The challenge of balancing philosophy and politics, as Vattimo himself confides, is one to which he has yet to find a "satisfactory solution."[3] Yet a resolution emerges within the development of his "ontology of actuality" and the transformation of philosophy into an ethics of interpretation.

Vattimo's initial "decision to study philosophy was largely a consequence of [his] religious commitment and [his] militant political attitude,"[4] which in the decade after the end of World War

II led Vattimo to write for a number of political journals and to participate in movements such as "Catholic Action." While Vattimo's political commitments in the 1950s predate his study of philosophy at the University of Turin, his encounter with his philosophical mentor, Luigi Pareyson, develops and shapes his understanding of the connection that ontology and hermeneutics have with political action. During World War II, Pareyson was an active member of the *Partito d'Azione* and the broader antifascist resistance movement in the Piedmont region of Italy. With many of his former *liceo* students actively involved in the resistance, Pareyson conducted lessons on philosophy and politics with selected graduates, instructing them so that they could spread the antifascist doctrine through the Action Party's underground publications. Pareyson wrote philosophical, as well as political, essays and texts at this time, and was eventually arrested (and quickly released) in 1944, whereupon his teaching was suspended until the end of the war.[5] Nonetheless, Pareyson looked skeptically upon his pupil's direct involvement with the religious and political movements of the day: due to its ontological character, philosophy was already and necessarily intertwined with all human activities, politics included.

This attitude is most pronounced in Pareyson's theoretical masterpiece, *Verità e interpretazione* (1971). Throughout the mid-1960s, Vattimo worked closely with his mentor on the lectures that form the theoretical core of Pareyson's hermeneutic ontology. The title of Pareyson's 1964 autumn lecture, "Expressive Thought and Revelatory Thought," represents "the idea that thinking is itself a thinking of Being in both the objective and the subjective sense," whereby revelatory thought is able to interpret Being as a new opening of truth, while expressive thought is merely able to articulate particular truths from within an already established aperture.[6] Pareyson insists that philosophy "worthy of the name" is simultaneously revelatory and expressive. Vattimo develops and transforms this same distinction into a more profound and ultimately postmetaphysical recognition of the radically historical and eventlike character of Being and its multitude of forms. So while Vattimo agrees with Pareyson that the revelation of Being can only ever occur through its historical expression in the form of an interpretation, Vattimo rejects the still latent metaphysical commitments in Pareyson's "tragic thought," which thinks Being under the category of reality, rather than necessity, and "carries in itself the indelible trace of an originary conflict" between the choice for Being or non-Being.[7] Vattimo calls this "the last great metaphysical misunderstanding of Christian thinking, namely, the idea that there is a radical separation between the history of salvation and secular history by virtue of which the meaning of revelation would be exclusively apocalyptic."[8] Tragic thought requires an unquestioning reverence for an ontological origin that is wholly other and inexhaustible. Vattimo's revision—inspired by his Nietzschean reading of Heidegger—brings this very origin into the flux of history and prepares the way for an ontology of actuality that takes up the present moment as an origin to be emancipated from the essentialisms of metaphysics.

Understood as a way to dissolve philosophy into ethics and "consume" the theoretical experience of metaphysics,[9] the ontology of actuality carries a twofold significance: "making oneself aware of the paradigm into which one has been thrown" yet "suspending its claim to definitive validity and heeding Being as that which remains unsaid" (32). One reconstructs the sites of ontology in the present while resisting the temptation to consider "the self-consumption of truth in solidarity [as] an objective description of our situation" (134). Here one finds an alternative to the purported dilemma facing Vattimo's hermeneutics: its origin is neither metaphysical, since it resists any claim to ultimate validity or description, nor purely political, since its motivation is precisely the critique and rejection of simple will to power based on an ideal of charity. The alternative to the seemingly irresolvable dilemma between philosophy and politics is their dissolution into a way of thinking and acting that takes truth as a project for humanity rather than as its ultimate criterion.

The linchpin that unifies this double critique is Being, or more precisely, the ontological difference as a historical inheritance whose origin is present to us only through an interpretation in the here and now. There is no ultimate appeal to Being as the ineffable source of reality; rather, for Vattimo we are always already underway and thrown into a historical context. Thus, the truth of human freedom is not originary as it was for Pareyson (Being is the originary choice for existence, as spelled out in his emblematic *Ontology of Freedom*)[10] but is something we construct through the remembering of ontological difference—what Vattimo often refers to as the *andenkend* thought of Heidegger, which has "no origin placed somewhere outside of the actuality of the event" (42). Pareyson's metaphysical insistence on the originary choice for Being and truth—a "for or against" alternative—represents a species of ontological blackmail no longer tenable if one accepts the end of metaphysics. The ontology of actuality willingly lets go of this final metaphysical limitation and accepts plurality and community, rather than originary conflict, as the trace of Being.

At the end of the second section of *Truth and Interpretation*, entitled "Ideology and Truth," Pareyson addresses the problematic relation between politics and philosophy, claiming that a philosopher who engages in politics is merely the product of a "contingent and accidental personal union" and that a philosopher "must do philosophy and nothing else, and right there one finds his civil task and his political relevance."[11] Under the rubric of an ontology of actuality, Vattimo transforms the contingent nature of the philosopher's union with politics into a vocation—a response to the destiny of Being as its weakening, recovery, and distortion through which the exceptionality of philosophy and politics is dissolved into ethics. Thus, when Vattimo asks, "what becomes of the philosophy-politics relation in a world in which . . . politics can no longer be thought of in terms of truth?" (41), the task of the philosopher dissolves into ethics and is charged with the responsibility that accompanies every interpretation: to listen, to be charitable, and most of all, to take seriously the risk that accompanies every construction of truth.

In this light, the three prescriptions for the philosopher-politician suggested by Pareyson in *Truth and Interpretation* take on a "weakened" or nihilistic character. The first commits the philosopher to hermeneutic truth over any ideological commitment that ignores ontological difference; the second warns that philosophy should not furnish criteria for political choices and serve as an expert authority external to practice. These two poles mirror the aforementioned false dilemma that challenges Vattimo's hermeneutics: "On the one side, the idea that thought precedes action, where practice is lowered to pure and simple 'application' of theory, which is a form of dogmatism or fanaticism; and on the other side, the idea that action precedes thought, where theory becomes the lowly instrument of practice, that is, a form of skepticism or cynicism."[12] However, Vattimo also understands that the philosopher-politician's relation to truth can no longer be tied to a notion of exceptionality or expertise that serves as an ultimate ground always beyond the reach of interpretation. Vattimo's ground (if we can speak of one) is itself an interpretation, a never fully given and historical inheritance that provides the philosopher-politician with the context for an ethics. No longer is the philosopher to be the advisor of princes, nor the instrument of the state; the philosopher's position is "privileged" only to the extent that she, in the manner that Nietzsche suggests, is able to lift herself periodically above the raging waters of history and be "untimely."

Vattimo therefore interprets Pareyson's third prescription as a call to dissolve philosophy into ethics: "If philosophy is the *verbal and speculative* translation of revelatory and ontological thought, its task is to vindicate the revelatory and ontological nature that every human activity, including practical action, can have in itself."[13] Vattimo's ontology of actuality retains the force of this vindication; yet, it is neither a political and thus ultimately dogmatic move that unashamedly prefers one vision of life over another, nor is it, on the other hand, a metaphysical move that seeks its ground in an absolute truth or description of reality. Only as a response to a particular historical opening—what Vattimo argues here is the epochal truth of democracy—does the confluence of philosopher and politician emerge as a vocation to make history by interpreting, and thus constructing, the truth.

The full force of this demand is registered in the short collection of reflections entitled *La vocazione e responsabilità del filosofo*

(2000), where Vattimo claims that the political life of the philosopher is neither contrived nor something that one merely falls into; rather, it is a choice for human liberation that places pedagogy before ideology, the transformation of individual minds before the transformation of the shape of society.[14] Yet one could justifiably critique the impetus, as well as the efficacy, of this philosophical mode of political activism. Vattimo recounts that as the events of 1968 were coming to a head in Europe, Pareyson commented about the students occupying the Sorbonne: "I am much more revolutionary than they are." Vattimo adds: "I knew just what he meant and felt the same way, because we were reading Heidegger and thinking about metaphysics and how it had to end, and these in their way were projects for radical transformation."[15] But is it enough to read Heidegger? Is merely "doing philosophy"—let alone Heideggerian ontology—radical enough when it is warranted, if not downright necessary, to confront directly the array of fundamentalisms that threaten the democratic ideals of plurality, solidarity, and freedom?

If Pareyson's solution preserves the purity and the unity of philosophy in the face of challenges from other realms of human activity, Vattimo's dissolution of philosophy and politics into ethics represents not only a step beyond his master but an indication of just how "accomplished" Vattimo's nihilism is. Philosophy and politics are historical projects, and "the basis of any historical project must be negation of the violence that is the heritage of metaphysics, negation of conservatism and domination under the pretexts of truth, the datum, order" (110). In relation to politics, then, the philosopher is not merely the custodian of Being but employs a form of anarchical thinking (literally, one that shakes up the various *archai*)[16] that Vattimo argues—borrowing loosely from Reiner Schürmann's reading of Heidegger—is able to remember Being by suspending the present order's claim to validity. In other words, the philosopher-politician embraces nihilism as a vocation.

The portrait of this philosopher-politician provides a powerful lens through which one can view the particular relevance of *Farewell to Truth*. Vattimo notes that democracy, understood as an epochal event, is marked by two significant events in the last century: what Heidegger describes as the "end of metaphysics" and the collapse of socialism that gives rise to particularly concrete and pragmatic forms of liberalism. Vattimo even claims that the end of metaphysics has its political parallel in the strengthening of democracy, as the subsequent swapping of party ideology for a model of political consensus is more akin to a play of forces than to an adherence to some absolute "truth." The interpretation of democracy (loosely construed) as the dominant horizon of political, social, and economic life after metaphysics nonetheless reveals the ultimately "moderate" character of Vattimo's politics. Whether we associate this stance with Nietzsche's "Good European," Rorty's notion of "commonsense Heideggerianism," or even Kant's employment of regulative ideals,[17] the rubric that guides Vattimo's hermeneutics is neither (as the critique of hermeneutic theories often is) simple tradition and respect for authority and authenticity, nor the simple conflict of interpretations, but rather the basic understanding that one can no longer appeal to essences of any kind as a ground for philosophical truth or political action.

In Vattimo's estimation, defenders of democracy like Habermas and Apel remain trapped within just such a metaphysical model by attempting to legitimate democracy through an appeal to reason and the essential truths that can be derived from it. The argument for (or perhaps more accurately, *of*) democracy brings Vattimo's thinking to a plurality of sites open for revision and interpretation. The first, as suggested above, is Heidegger and the contentious legacy that surrounds his thought. Vattimo's new trajectory breaks from the strict coordinates of Nietzsche and Heidegger by placing them into a broader (and somewhat contrived) constellation of thinkers who challenge the supremacy of absolute truth. Thus Heidegger's "The End of Philosophy and the Task of Thought" and Popper's *The Open Society and Its Enemies* are read together as rejections of Platonism and, consequently, challenges to the essentialism and authoritarianism of metaphysical thinking. And while this might on the surface appear to be a deliberate strategy intended to mitigate the thornier political issues associated with Heidegger, his recovery and conversion is possible because of a transformation in thinking. Philosophy can transform the world, rather than just contemplate it, because it is no longer allied with an absolute notion of truth and teaches us that our position is a finite and historical one. If one condemns Heidegger's Nazism, one must do it for the same reasons that one condemns (as Adorno did) the continuation of totalitarianism in the world of advertising and market propaganda, the imposition of religious ideology by militant extremists, and the forceful exportation of democracy around the world.

For similar reasons, Vattimo, invoking Heidegger's famous comment to *Der Spiegel*, suggests that only a "relativistic" or "kenotic" God can save us. The central role that religion plays today in political and scientific discourses underscores the particular relevance of Vattimo's new reflections on his already developed notion of a weakened or *verwunden* Christianity. The subjective and interpretative nature of Christianity will welcome the "fare-well" to objective truth only when it finally accepts that "the death of god proclaimed by Nietzsche is nothing more than the death of Jesus on the cross" (58). Unfortunately, the Catholic Church remains where it was when it condemned Galileo—convinced of the true "nature" and "essence" of reality such that it can derive norms from what are merely facts of the world. Until the Church embraces the idea, already present in St. Paul's "truth-speaking," that truth is something we construct, it will continue to have issues with homosexuality, gender equality, the proper use of biotechnology, and so on because they threaten the Church's vision of what the world is supposed to be. For Vattimo, Christianity begins with a break from what is perceived to be "natural": above all else, to love one's enemies is *not* what nature prescribes. This awareness also helps to mitigate calls to recognize the Christian identity of Europe (no doubt in the face of ever-increasing populations of non-Christian Europeans). The European Union, itself an artificial union from the start, can benefit from its Christian heritage only if it is interpreted as "a potent summons to disidentification" (81).

Vattimo's recommendations hold great promise on the other side of the Atlantic, where calls to reinforce the fact that the United States is a Christian nation reflect a similar ideological push against tolerance, inclusion, and dialogue. In fact, the issue of Christian identity seems but one aspect of a broader and consistent appeal to essential natures in politics (one need only consider those who question President Obama's citizenship), whereby the working myth is that the essence of what "America" or "the West" is faces inevitable ruin from hostile forces. The prevailing response on the left and the right in American politics and media—whether the issue is immigration, the war on terror, or health care—centers on various forms of American exceptionalism, and *mutatis mutandis*, American sovereignty at home and around the world. And while it would certainly be appropriate to accuse the American right of distorting Heidegger's comment to read "only a decider can save us now," the left's recent appeal to "hope" and "change we can believe in" has also failed to produce any real economic and political pluralism at home and abroad.

At fault is what Nietzsche describes in section 241 of *Beyond Good and Evil* as "soil addiction."[18] In the difficult chapter "On Peoples and Fatherlands" (sections 240–256), Nietzsche undertakes a geographical (rather than genealogical) revaluing of values in the attempt to undermine the persistent claim (so present in early theories on race and in various forms of "social Darwinism") that certain characteristics are necessarily found in peoples of certain geographical regions. This technique is also employed in section 329 of Nietzsche's *Gay Science*, entitled "Leisure and Idleness":

> There is something of the American Indian, something of the savagery peculiar to the Indian blood, in the way the Americans strive for gold; and their breathless haste in working—the true vice of the new world—is already starting to spread to old Europe, making it savage and covering it with a most odd mindlessness. Already one is ashamed of keeping still; long reflection almost gives people a bad conscience.[19]

Nietzsche's broad point is that the "Americanness" of Americans (and one might surmise today, the European Union) has nothing at all to do with geography or race and everything to do with the construction of that truth as an *ethos* (in this case, a violent ethos that, now in the age of democracy and relative comfort, requires "a really different humanity for these new conditions, equal to the new situation").[20] To mistake a constructed truth for an essential quality—insert your favorite politician's appeal to American ingenuity, or tenacity, or values—is the heart of exceptionalism, a *"crude obviousness"* in all endeavors whereby "the feeling for form itself" and "the melody of movements"[21] is lost.

Vattimo's recent call to "re-become" a communist is an attempt to construct a new *ethos* and break the eternal return of the political pendulum (where left and right have little difference) by challenging democracies everywhere to reject the appeal to essences.[22] The most pernicious of these absolutes, and the one at which Vattimo directs his most potent arguments here and in *Ecce Comu*, is the free market. Along with Being, it seems that Western democracies have forgotten Marx's central claim that political economy is not a natural science. Vattimo notes that in late capitalism the promulgation of markets seems to resemble the same type of weakening distortion that one sees at the end of metaphysics. The challenge is therefore not to overcome capitalism but to work through its forms and mitigate the claims that the absolute faith in the free market often makes in the face of real poverty and alienation.

Vattimo also brings Marx into the fold of Nietzsche and Heidegger and the attempt to think the ontological difference, a project he first attempted with his works *Il soggetto e la maschera* (1974) and *Al di là del soggetto* (1981). While real Marxism has suffered because of its commitment to natural essences, Vattimo preserves Marx's critique of ideology and his understanding of alienation in order to resuscitate Marx's eleventh thesis on

Feuerbach: that the task of philosophy is not to interpret the world but to transform it. Vattimo rereads this thesis alongside Heidegger's claim that "science does not think." Together, these ideas present a potent critique of philosophy as a specialized and "expert" discipline among others. If this is an epoch when philosophy can transform the world and thus become an ethics of interpretation, thinking democracy must above all entail the thinking of difference rather than the thinking of equality and essences.

As a political gesture, the thinking of difference turns its attention away from the *obviousness* of the simply present and toward its absence. Difference in its most basic form is always present through the absence of essence. That which differs from me, my way of life, my gender, my species, and so on challenges my perceived essence through its very negation. The ontology of actuality takes up the thinking of difference with the imperative to avoid its own absolutization and overconceptualization (as if there were an "essence" of difference). The unfolding of *attualità*, the present moment, *is* difference, and it seems that any other sort of ontology would be condemned to treat its objects as fixed truths or as abstractions. The image of a mechanical river of bottles speeding by on a production line illustrates how the present negates itself through the continual passing of its moments, even with the appearance of sameness. It is not surprising that Chaplin's *Modern Times* is one of Vattimo's favorite references when speaking of the dangers of capitalism and technology. To be caught up in the system is to be lost in a series of essences: alienated, reduced, and equated. The *movement and form* of the present is the movement of dialectic and negation, but in its weakened sense. Through the thought of difference we find that we are always-already alienated, and the task of the ontology of actuality, of ethics, is to reinvigorate the present and bring it up for questioning and interpretation.

In the midst of alienation and negation Vattimo returns to a weakened form of Hegelianism. Vattimo revises his claim from the late 1980s that the expansion of various media into all facets of life has produced a general aestheticization of experience, one so thoroughgoing that it appears not as the concretization of Hegelian Spirit but as its caricature. Vattimo's appraisal in *Farewell* is that we must return to Hegel again because there we will find a correlate to the neopragmatic understanding of democracy and truth that Vattimo shares with Rorty. Spirit unfolds not as a progress toward its ultimate realization but as an ever-unfolding and "never totally given, overcoming of every form of alienation" (140). To revise Hegel's *Philosophy of Right*, where the individual is finally recognized in the State, we could perhaps understand democracy as the never-to-be-completed State, the one that is never real, resists its reduction to essence, and attempts to construct the recognition of the other in the State.

Vattimo recognizes that a democratic project for humanity is "artificial" and constructed rather than based on "natural" essences, and his intellectual and personal biography reads like a careful and sustained interpretation of the shared inheritance of Western society, a response to the protracted and long-overdue farewell to truth. Rather than find truth at the base of authentic human coexistence, Vattimo embraces "the capacity to listen, the respect for the equal freedom of every person (individuals, groups, communities) that is the better legacy of Western culture, betrayed today by those who pretend to be its bearers."[23]

This antiauthoritarian orientation has deep roots in Vattimo's thinking, a guiding thread that extends from his radical and emancipatory interpretation of Nietzsche in the 1970s to *Hermeneutic Communism*, his forthcoming collaboration with Santiago Zabala. *Farewell to Truth* does not mark a new direction in Vattimo's thinking, nor is it a specialized form of applied philosophy that rises and falls with the tides of the latest crises. One could rightly say that by achieving the end of philosophy in ethics and politics—by accomplishing nihilism—Vattimo finally (to steal a phrase from Nietzsche) "becomes who he truly is."[24] Vattimo's stance is neither that truth has been lost nor that we should bid it good riddance; rather, his suggestion is that our 2,500-year love affair with truth has run its course. The situation demands that we set truth free, and in so doing, free ourselves.

NOTES

1. Gianni Vattimo, *Beyond Interpretation*, trans. David Webb (Stanford, Calif.: Stanford University Press, 1997), 1.

2. I am thinking primarily of Paolo Flores D'Arcais, who suggests that Vattimo's motivation is ultimately and unavoidably a political one. Cf. "Gianni Vattimo, or Rather: Hermeneutics as the Primacy of Politics," in *Weakening Philosophy: Festschrift in Honor of Professor Gianni Vattimo*, ed. Santiago Zabala (Montreal: McGill-Queen's University Press, 2007), 250–269.

3. Gianni Vattimo, Luca Savarino, and Federico Vercellone, "Gianni Vattimo: Philosophy as Ontology of Actuality," *Iris* 1, no. 2 (October 2009): 343.

4. Ibid., 312.

5. For many of the details related to this period of Pareyson's life, I am indebted to the chronology of events assembled by Francesco Tomatis in *Pareyson: Vita, filosofia, bibliographia* (Brescia: Editrice Morcelliana, 2003).

6.   Vattimo, Savarino, and Vercellone, "Gianni Vattimo," 319–320.

7.   Gianni Vattimo, "Pareyson: From Aesthetics to Ontology" in *Art's Claim to Truth*, trans. Luca D'Isanto (New York: Columbia University Press, 2008). Cf. also Luigi Pareyson, "Pensiero ermeneutico e pensiero tragico," in *Dove va la filosofia italiana?* Ed. J. Jacobelli (Roma-Bari: Laterza, 1986), 137.

8.   Gianni Vattimo, *Belief*, trans. Luca D'Isanto (Stanford, Calif.: Stanford University Press, 1999), 81.

9.   Gianni Vattimo, "Ontology of Actuality," in *Contemporary Italian Philosophy: Crossing the Borders of Ethics, Politics, and Religion*, ed. Silvia Benso and Brian Schroeder (Albany, N.Y.: SUNY Press, 2007), 105.

10. Luigi Pareyson, *Ontologia della libertà. Il male e la sofferenza* (Torino: Einaudi, 1995).

11. Luigi Pareyson, *Verità e interpretazione* (Milano: Mursia, 1971), 178.

12. Ibid., 183.

13. Pareyson, *Verità e interpretazione*, 185.

14. Gianni Vattimo, *The Responsibility of the Philosopher*, trans. William McCuaig (New York: Columbia University Press, 2010), 109.

15. Ibid., 110.

16. I contend elsewhere that Vattimo's thinking creates an "archaic" confusion and places the various first principles of competing discourses into conversation. Cf. Robert Valgenti, "Gianni Vattimo's Recovery of Reason," in *Between Nihilism and Politics: The Hermeneutics of Gianni Vattimo*, ed. Silvia Benso and Brian Schroeder (Albany, N.Y.: SUNY Press, 2010).

17. Vattimo makes note of this connection when he discusses the universality of political projects as a construction rather than as an appeal to an absolute: "The idea of universality as a construct, of the universal as task or project or guiding idea—the idea fundamentally driving all of philosophical culture since Kant—must be bound rigorously to a political project. Indeed, it demands to be recognized as a political construct to all intents and purposes." *The Responsibility of the Philosopher*, 116–117.

18. Cf. Friedrich Nietzsche, *Beyond Good and Evil: Prelude to a Philosophy of the Future*, trans. Judith Norman (Cambridge: Cambridge University Press, 2001), 132.

19. Friedrich Nietzsche, *The Gay Science*, trans. Josefine Nauckhoff (Cambridge: Cambridge University Press, 2001), 183.

20. Gianni Vattimo, *Il soggetto e la maschera. Nietzsche e il problema della liberazione* (Fabbri-Bompiani, 1974), 116.

21. Ibid., 184. Similar ideas, such as the "plastic power" and sense of "style," are central to Vattimo's reading of Nietzsche's second *Untimely Meditation*.

22. Gianni Vattimo, *Ecce Comu* (Rome: Fazi, 2007).

23. Ibid., 38.

24. The subtitle of *Ecce Comu* plays upon this idea, which reads: "How to re-become what one was."

A FAREWELL TO TRUTH: I have chosen this paradoxical title because it conveys something important about theoretical and philosophical aspects of our culture now, and also about everyday experience. As far as the latter goes, it is increasingly clear to all and sundry that "the media lie" and that everything is turning into a game of interpretations—not disinterested, not necessarily false, but (and this is the point) oriented toward projects, expectations, and value choices at odds with one another. The culture of countries in the West is becoming, as a matter of fact, though often not in law, more pluralistic all the time. The outcome of the war in Iraq has forced the leaders of the major governments who ordered the invasion of that country to admit that they lied to their publics, and whether they did so voluntarily or involuntarily is an unresolved problem on which no light will ever be shed by the supposedly independent inquiries that they themselves have set up. These admissions have highlighted once again the question of what truth might be in politics. Many of us have had to register the fact that the scandal attaching to Bush and Blair over their lies about Saddam's weapons of mass destruction was not in the least pure and objective, which is how they tend to portray it. But let's ask ourselves: if Bush and Blair had lied just as shamelessly for a noble cause, for example in order to reduce the cost of the drugs used to treat AIDS in the world's poor countries, would we be just as scandalized? It is no secret that far worse violations (on the part of the intelligence services, for example) are accepted as necessary when it comes to national defense. As I found out when I was a member of the European Parliament committee studying the Echelon system, which indiscriminately intercepts electronic communications worldwide through a satellite network operated by the United States, Great Britain, Canada, New Zealand, and Australia, we are under surveillance by a Big Brother who is not in the least imaginary and acts at the behest of the United States and its closest allies. This surveillance is illegal for the most part, but even the European Union can't do anything about it, since questions of national security (but who decides what those are?) remain the preserve of the individual governments, who shrink from taking a stand against the American superpower. Naturally I am well aware that complex Western societies have a security problem, because their technological infrastructure leaves them vulnerable. But what looks less and less convincing is the way that the United States thinks that it can solve this problem for itself and for the rest of the world, which it doesn't even bother to consult.

This example goes to show how politics and politicians today are allowed many ethical violations, including violations of the duty to tell the truth, without scandalizing anyone. And anyway, even the potentially "good" reasons for Bush and Blair to lie about Iraq ought to make us think. Tolerance of untruth has been present and accepted since the dawn of time in practical politics, but it was seen as a violation deserving censure in the realm of ethics: the whole story of modern political Machiavellianism is there in a nutshell. Today, though, it is paralleled in philosophy (or, rather, in a good many philosophies, not all) by the demise of the very idea of truth. This decline of the idea of objective truth in philosophy and epistemology doesn't yet seem to have floated to the surface of public consciousness, which is still deeply attached, as the scandal clinging to the "liars" Bush and Blair shows, to the idea of the true as the objective description of the facts. It's a bit like what happens with heliocentrism: all of us still say the sun is going down, even if it's the Earth that is rotating. Or better, like what Nietzsche said about God: he has died, but plenty of people haven't heard the news yet. Or Heidegger's message that metaphysics is over but can't be overcome, maybe only *verwunden*.

The decline of truth may be illustrated with a couple of examples from Adorno and Heidegger. The first is the significance of Adorno's reprise and dissolution of the notion of dialectic. According to Adorno, dialectic has two essential meanings: totality and reappropriation. Hence we do not observe the truth because we cannot observe the total, and ideology is false consciousness, because partial. Alienation itself is partiality. Reappropriation, on the other hand, means grasping the whole, seeing how it hangs together, not letting oneself be fooled by appearance. But Adorno already recognizes, as does Heidegger to an even greater degree, that totality does not reappropriate precisely because it is, in principle and increasingly in fact, realized. "The whole is the untrue" (*das Ganze ist das Umwahre*) reads a famous sentence from Adorno's *Minima Moralia* (1951). The (tendentially complete) attainment of instrumental rationality in mass society may realize totality, but it does so in a way that is the opposite of liberatory. Adorno runs into a theoretical impasse here, because the ideal of truth-liberation is supposed to be that of totality achieved.

Sartre encounters a similar impasse, but he makes further strides: in his *Critique of Dialectical Reason* (1960) he advances the notion that alienation will end when the meaning of our actions, which we do not possess because we live in the society of the division of labor and class domination, will be the common possession of all actors. But this shared possession, which comes about in so-called groups in fusion, the revolutionary community in the heat of battle seizing the Winter Palace, doesn't last. The "practical-inert," as Sartre calls it, fastens its grip and reimposes divisions of the kind familiar from Soviet-style bureaucracy; common possession of truth quickly evaporates. Yet totality remains the overriding value.

What impelled Adorno to criticize massified totality? The same thing that drove Levinas or Benjamin: micrological pathos, *pietas* for the offense to life. Negative dialectic is a vindication of the irreducibility of this offended existence with respect to totality. From it the whole aesthetics of Adorno follows, including his theory of the avant-garde, with its silence, its incomprehensibility. Just a *promesse de bonheur*, never grasped for more than a fleeting moment. No "death of art," either in Hegel or in Benjamin. A sequel to that is the attitude typical of revolutionary thought post-1968, which becomes tragic thought in many cases. In this dialectical perspective, which remains the one most expressive of modernity and which had already surpassed in many senses the more or less ingenuous idea of an objective mirroring of things in themselves (undermined since Kant and his transcendental philosophy but revived to some extent in Hegel), truth is the vision that escapes the partiality imposed by the conditions of social exploitation or even just by the limitations of individual and class interest. But this remains an objective vision, precisely because not partial. What is new in Adorno is that he realizes that this totality, which appears to be the sole possibility of access to truth, is the polar opposite of the liberty that ought to accompany truth.

In Heidegger too, however paradoxical it might seem, the motives for the dissolution of truth are the same—even if the philosopher from Messkirch goes beyond the straightforward reduction of the true to an utterly negative utopian ideal. Adorno kept faith with the objectivistic ideal of the true as totality dialectically unfolded, which was already the ideal of Hegel and Marx. But in becoming aware that such an ideal demanded a social transformation that could only end in totalitarianism, he in fact liquidated it, reducing it to the aesthetic momentariness that also characterizes Sartre's discourse. Both Adorno and Sartre acknowledge, but only implicitly, that the ideal of truth-totality contains within itself depths of violence. And as far as that goes, think of the two extremes of the history of philosophy: Aristotle, whose *Metaphysics* begins with the affirmation that knowledge is knowing everything and that this goal can be reached by knowing the first causes (which enables us to dominate events, however), and Nietzsche, for whom "metaphysics is the claim to seize control by force of the most fertile territories" (the causes once again, which permit us to dominate things).

Certainly, in Heidegger's attack on metaphysics (which commences in 1927 with *Being and Time*, although there he targets only the idea of truth as correspondence, as faithful description of the facts) the crucial motif is once again, albeit implicitly, the violence it entails. Heidegger shares the concerns of the early twentieth-century avant-garde as we find them expressed in Ernst Bloch, for example, or subsequently in Charlie Chaplin's *Modern Times*. The fear was that objectivistic metaphysics grounded in the idea of truth as correspondence (culminating in positivism) was preparing for (or bringing about) the advent of a society of total organization. Only this avant-garde (and fundamentally existentialist) inspiration accounts for Heidegger's polemic against truth as correspondence, for it would be absurd to think that what makes him deny this vision of truth, and of Being itself, is the drive to find a more objectively valid definition. It is interesting that Heidegger too, in a lecture from the 1960s published in *Zur Sache des Denkens* (1969), appears to be thinking not just the notion of truth but the task of thought in general in terms that refer back to totality. His summons not to rest content with the "ongoing presentation of that which is present as *Vorhandenes*" ("*vorhandenen Gegenwärtigung des Anwesenden*" [1969, 79]) recalls, and not just on the surface, the Marxist critique of ideology—the "school of suspicion." The task of thought is to seize, not forget, that which remains concealed in the "ongoing presentation" of what eventuates, meaning, for Adorno, as for Marx (and Hegel), the dialectical concreteness of the links that ideology hides from us. For Heidegger, in contrast, it is truth as *aletheia*, as the opening of a horizon (or paradigm) that enables the truth of statements that conform to things, the truth of propositions verified or falsified. Heidegger would never believe, though, that to "think" the opening within which individual truths are given (the propositions that can be verified or falsified on the basis of it) amounted to gaining cognizance of an ulterior, more ample truth. One of the sayings for which he is known is that "science doesn't think." In Kantian terms, science recognizes (the phenomenon) but does not grasp the noumenon, and it is the noumenon that is "thought." The model of totality, which appears to inspire his appeal not to forget that which lies beyond, and behind, the simply-present, the *Vorhandenes*, is not a strictly cognoscitive appeal. Obviously it isn't that in Marx and Adorno either, at any rate in the sense that for them it is possible to appropriate the truth of the total only on the basis of a practical alteration of society. But this revolutionary transformation remains merely the premise for something that is, ultimately, objective cognizance. Here, in Marxism itself, lies the seed of the failure of communist society: on the premise that a tendentially scientific knowledge of the laws of society and economy has been attained, the division is reestablished between those who really know, the central committee, and the "empiric proletariat," those without access to such knowledge. In Adorno, the cognoscitive model exerts less pressure, because he had the failure of communist society before his eyes: there remains only a negative horizon, which leads him to shift the end of alienation onto the plane of utopia, entrusting it solely to the *promesse de bonheur* of aesthetic experience.

Heidegger, who resists letting himself be overwhelmed by the longstanding domination of the model of objective truth, conducts a discourse that, in the end, seems to respond better to the demands of dialectical thought, in the sense that it takes fully on board that upending of philosophy into praxis which Marx envisioned but did not completely achieve, because of the persistence of a scientistic and objectivistic vision of truth. The practical transformation of the conditions of existence, to state a paradox, is taken more seriously by Heidegger than by Marx. The relation of thought to the truth of Being, to the original aperture of truth, to the milieu into which *Dasein* is thrown, is in no sense a cognizance, a theoretical acquisition. Rather, it is what Wittgenstein would call the sharing of a "form of life." This does not mean something purely irrational, since, in Heidegger anyway, it means assuming the heritage of the tradition into which we are thrown as a horizon of possibility. This may seem circular, but if it is, it is a hermeneutic circle, not a vicious one. We may enter into a relation with the situation into which we are thrown in two ways: by conceiving it as a datum to be known objectively or as a message that we have to knowingly interpret and transform. The first attitude is no more than a scientistic, metaphysical illusion supposedly capable of articulation on the basis of the (objective, descriptive) truth of the datum, of the story that leads to me. It is the inauthentic assumption of the past as *vergangen* and not as *gewesen* (here I advert to the pages of *Being and Time*). But to assume the past as *gewesen*—as a having-been that still presents as the possibility of deciding freely—means accepting history as open to the future, as something incapable of being encapsulated in a true knowledge, even that of the revolutionary proletariat.

At this point, the meaning of the title *Farewell to Truth* comes into sharper focus. Leave is taken of truth as the objective mirroring of a datum that, to be adequately described, must be fixed and stable—must literally be "a given" (which is what the word *datum* means). That is feasible in the sciences that "don't think," because they do not query the horizon (the paradigm) that envelops them and because they ignore the totality of the dialectical relations that condition their objects. A problem like the one that I alluded to above, of lying in politics, clearly fits into this context. If I say that the lies of Bush and Blair don't matter to me as long as they were justified by good intentions, meaning ones I share, I accept that the truth about the facts is a matter of interpretation, conditional upon a shared paradigm. That this sounds like Machiavellianism pure and simple I quite realize. But Machiavelli's mistake (to put it in simple terms, since his thought is a lot more complex than that) perhaps lies merely in having left the faculty of lying, or of violating other moral imperatives, exclusively to the prince. Gramsci, I recall, said that in the modern world, the prince was the political party, and that in itself was a step in the direction of democracy, even if the party was not yet society *in toto*.

It is a perilous step, evidently, analogous to that of Lukács when he imagines that the "empiric" proletariat is not identical to the "transcendental," authentic proletariat—the party and its leadership. These are all ways of widening the application of Machiavelli's principle to cover more ground and so fundamentally constitute advances toward greater democracy. But they always retain the limitation of supposing ulterior truth to be the metaphysical object of an intuition available only to a subject—a subject qualified in some manner to receive it, in other words the prince, distinct from the collectivity in general, even when identified as a collective subject. Such a limitation signals to me that these authors have not yet fully acquiesced in a truly laic conception of the State. They are unable to see that the truth that matters in politics—and in every other field—is not objective correspondence but the paradigmatic horizon within which every correspondence is verifiable.

What we might call the epistemological precondition of social and intercultural dialogue is precisely this truth of horizon which politics has the task of grasping and attempting to make explicit and to construct. From this there follow important consequences for how we conceive politics and its truth. One is a radical retreat from all claims to ground politics in some scientific discipline, even economics or technology. One recalls, in passing, that one of the major themes of Marx at his best was the negation of the thesis that political economy is a natural science. The same stricture applies to the claim to know the truth about human rights, and to base policies of just war and humanitarian intervention on this true cognizance of the truth, without taking into account the cultural paradigms of others. These factual, so to speak "objectual," truths hold good in politics only if they are legitimate within the horizon of the paradigm. Philosophers and intellectuals, following a pattern that basically derives from figures like Socrates—and from the sophists too, however much the divine Plato scorns them—labor on the plane of these "horizontal" truths, in an attempt to render a form of life more comprehensible, more shared, more argued over, and more emotionally participative.

So today, much more clearly than in the past, the question of truth is recognized as a question of interpretation, of the application of paradigms that, in turn, are not objective (since no one verifies or falsifies them except on the basis of other paradigms) but that are a matter of social sharing. The exception that Machiavelli granted to the prince was basically only a correlate of the power, which also belonged to the prince, to establish the canons of the true and the false, to establish what it was more or less obligatory to accept as true (one thinks of what Nietzsche had to say in "On Truth and Lies in a Nonmoral Sense," 1873).

The conclusion toward which I am working is that the farewell to truth is the commencement, and the very basis, of democracy. If there were an objective truth to social and economic laws (economics is not a natural science), democracy would be an utterly irrational choice. It would be better to entrust the management of the State to experts, to Plato's philosopher-kings or all the Nobel Prize winners in every category. A list of those who ultimately concur on these points would include Heidegger, Karl Popper (the foe of the closed Platonic society), Adorno himself, and Marx even earlier. Our pluralistic society continues to give credence to the metaphysical idea of truth as objective correspondence to the facts, as political debate proves day after day. It views interpretation as just interpretation and deludes itself that it can bring about agreement on the basis of factual data or even on the basis of the essential laws of nature. So we see the Italian Parliament passing laws on bioethics (embryos, assisted procreation, and so on) that impose on everyone a "natural" law that only the authority of the Roman Catholic Church deems such. The economy is managed in accordance with another supposedly natural law, that of the market and unlimited competition, and we see the result all around us in the current economic crisis. Truth faces a challenge in the world of postmodern pluralism—the challenge of coming to grips with the fact that consensus on individual questions is above all a problem of collective interpretation, of constructing paradigms shared or, at any rate, explicitly recognized. The parabola of the notion of truth in the twentieth century reveals a transition from truth to charity—a topic on which I shall expand. What Thomas Kuhn (1962) called paradigms are beliefs shared (ones tested by time, of course, and by experience gained within the framework they authorize) by entire societies or smaller communities, like those of physicists or theologians. It always comes down, in the end, to a question of belonging. Not "Plato a friend, but truth a greater friend" but rather "truth a friend, but (or: because) Plato a greater friend." I repeat: this is not a profession of irrationalism along the lines of: let us think according to what, biologically and historically, we already are, period! Why not? Because the provenance on the basis of which we formulate our judgments is not a closed and immutable past (the stony weight that oppressed Zarathustra); it is not a cause. But to the extent that it summons us and offers itself up to interpretation, it is always already a motive, an ensemble of messages, a language that speaks to us (and about us) and that we speak.

We have not yet elaborated all the implications for social life and politics that this philosophical perspective on truth entails. For example, it certainly opens the way to a more adequate consideration of our current media-saturated society, stripping away the legitimacy of any pretense to furnish the true truth and focusing attention on the background, on the unsaid that underlies any claim to objectivity. It also strips away any possible legitimacy from all those policies that propose setting limits to the freedom and the interests of all on the basis of a consideration of what is objectively necessary to a society: the free market must be protected even if it damages some groups, individuals, or classes; a resolute government must know how to make unpopular choices like participation in the Iraq war. Do I exaggerate the risk? We might not be facing the threat of a society like that depicted in *Modern Times* early in the twentieth century. But we are still oppressed by a fundamentalism of sorts, pretending to be defending us (our democracy, our way of life, our goods) regardless of what we the citizens either know or wish. In the end, it boils down to understanding that truth is not encountered but constructed with consensus and respect for the liberty of everyone, and the diverse communities that live together, without blending, in a free society.

To appeal to the Christian ideal of charity doesn't seem out of place, therefore. And a word used by Saint Paul, *aletheuontes* ("truth-speaking," which also turns up in book 6 of Aristotle's *Nicomachean Ethics*), may be taken in the strong sense, as a genuine invitation to construct a more "truthful" society, one freer, more democratic, more friendly.

A FAREWELL TO TRUTH

Karl Popper's ideas about the open society and its enemies, first published in a famous book in 1945, have become commonplace. But their extreme consequences are not always thought through. According to Popper, the enemies of the open society are all those theorists, starting with the philosophers in Plato's *Republic* who have emerged from the cave in which ordinary people dwell and have contemplated directly the eternal ideas of things (the truth of Being, not just its shadows). These Platonic philosophers have the right and the duty to go back down into the world and lead their fellows, or compel them if necessary, to recognize the truth. Counterintuitively, Popper puts modern philosophers like Hegel and Marx in Plato's company as enemies of the open society, despite the distance that separates their philosophies from Platonic idealism, for they too claim to ground politics in some truth. In Hegel's case, it is the truth of history that is realized providentially, apart from the intentions of the men and women who make it, by virtue of what he calls "the cunning of reason." In Marx's case, the truth is the revolution through which the proletariat (expropriated and alienated, and so enabled to see past the veils of interest that generate ideology to the truth) reconstitutes the totality, the profound truth, of the human essence and surpasses the social division of labor and the dominion of men over other men.

Popper's critique has been widely accepted by the whole modern liberal-democratic mentality, but not all of its logical implications as regards the relation between politics and truth have been perceived. If Popper is acknowledged to be right—as it seems to me that he must be—the obligatory conclusion is that truth itself is the enemy of the open society, and specifically of any democratic politics. Clearly, if we think truth as Popper thinks it—meaning a continuous process of trial and error, a process that, through the pure and simple falsification of hypotheses that are revealed to be ephemeral and unsustainable, frees us from erroneous representations without attaining definitive truths—his thesis has nothing controversial about it. Indeed, the democratic mentality has adopted it, but that doesn't seem to stop it from thinking that politics can still lay claim to some truth. The Anglo-American war against Iraq in the name of true democracy, which Westerners were meant to implant in that country by force, is an example of this ambiguity and this absence of radical critique. Neither Bush nor the neoconservatives who shaped White House policy rejected Popper's theses; indeed, they regarded his theory of the open society as one of their own founding principles. Yet they felt themselves entitled, like the philosophers in Plato's *Republic*, to steer the world, with force if necessary, toward the liberty that only the vision of truth can guarantee.

Such an ambiguity, which as the Iraq War example shows has very important practical consequences, is basically possible because Popper's own doctrine has not gone beyond the conception of truth as objectivity, as what medieval philosophy called *adaequatio intellectus et rei* (adequation between intellect and object), as the correspondence or "adequation" of mental representations to a real order imposed on reason to which reason must conform. Even the falsification of erroneous hypotheses, which Popper sets against the idea of knowledge as induction and the formulation of laws of universal validity, actually appears to advance progressively toward a given truth, which continues to function as a norm for thought. As long as truth is conceived as *adaequatio*, as correspondence to a given (a datum) objectively present, the danger of political Platonism never goes away. Obviously Karl Popper is not responsible for the Iraq fiasco. But the contradictions of democracy exported by force and even by preventive war require a critical rethink of the relation between politics and truth. To accomplish that, we need a notion of truth going far beyond the persistent realism of Popper and a great deal of contemporary philosophy. There is only one place from which to begin such a rethink, and that is the teachings of Nietzsche and Heidegger. It was they who fundamentally critiqued the notion of truth as objectivity and who, appearances and their own intentions to the contrary, laid the basis for a radical new vision of democracy itself.[1]

Nietzsche proposed an assessment of Western culture under the sign of nihilism. The result was schematically summarized in a famous section of *Twilight of the Idols* (1888) entitled "How the Real World at Last Became a Myth." At the outset, with Plato, the truth of things is located in the ideas, in those transcendental essences that serve as immutable models of the various realities and that guarantee the very possibility of speaking reasonably. Then, with Christianity, the truth of things is located in the world that awaits us after death, and we will only know it when we contemplate God there. Kant subsequently locates the seat of truth

in the mind, in the stable structures that reason employs to organize the world of phenomena, while remaining ignorant of how it
is "in itself." As the whole process draws to a close, Comte's scientific positivism comes on the scene to declare that only the fact
positively ascertained through the experimental method is truth,
but this fact is, as the word "fact" literally says, "made," produced
by the human subject endlessly modifying and manipulating
things. So truth comes to be identified, in Nietzsche's telling, with
that which mankind accomplishes in the world through technology; pure subjectivism triumphs, and there no longer exists any
independent objectivity, no "real world." Nietzsche, for his own
part, thinks that what exists is the pure conflictual interplay of
force and power, a conflict among interpretations with no moor-
ing in any objective norm that could decide truth. From 1927 on,
the year in which *Being and Time* appeared, Heidegger concurs in
many respects with this Nietzschean point of view. But he takes
Nietzsche to task for himself having remained a prisoner of the
idea of truth as objectivity. When this truth turns out to be unat-
tainable, Nietzsche is forced to fall back on a theory of the mere
ebb and flow of power. We all know how such emphasis on the play
of force was exploited by Nazism and fascism in the twentieth
century, going far beyond Nietzsche's original intention. What
Heidegger thinks is that we have the nihilistic outcome of Western philosophy right before our eyes, in the disappearance of the
"real world" and the onset in its place of the world of technological organization and industrial rationalization, in which man too
becomes a pure object of manipulation. This outcome follows directly from the metaphysical error of having imagined truth as
correspondence and Being as object. In other words, if one's point
of departure is the Platonic doctrine of the ideas, in which truth is

a stable, given order, to which the subject must make his or her own representations conform, the necessary point of arrival will be positivism and the world of untrammeled technological domination.

If the nightmare of "total organization" to which Adorno later alluded is to be avoided, Heidegger says, awareness must dawn that true Being is not an object. To use an image, we could say that true Being is instead the luminous medium within which objects appear to us, or to put it another way, the ensemble of presuppositions that make experience possible for us. In order to prove that a proposition really does correspond to a state of things, we require methods, criteria, models, which we need to have in place prior to any assay. In that regard, Heidegger speaks of a circle of comprehension-interpretation. The truth of single descriptive propositions depends on a more primordial truth, for which he chooses the term "opening" or "aperture" and by which he means that ensemble of presuppositions (and prejudices, of course) upon which depends any possibility of establishing correspondences between statements and things. I have already mentioned that the reason Heidegger, and with him a large part of existentialist thought in the twentieth century, especially the philosophical current today labeled hermeneutics, rejected and rejects the idea of truth as objectivity is ethicopolitical:[2] if true Being were only that which is objective, quantifiable, and given once and for all like the Platonic Ideas (to simplify Platonism drastically), our existence as free subjects would have no meaning; we could not say of ourselves that "we are," and on top of that, we would be exposed to the risk of totalitarianism. To really "be," we would have to abandon all our uncertainties, hopes, affects, and projects and match in every respect what social rationality demands of us, be perfect cogs in the evenly humming machinery of production, consumption, and reproduction. One thinks of Comte actually discussing industrial ethics and fancying that moral behavior ought to be modeled on the assembly line, where each one performs exactly what the others expect of him and doesn't hold up the production process.

So then, if there is no more real doubt that truth-as-object isn't good for us, the question arises: how exactly does this Heideggerian notion of truth as aperture represent something better, strictly from the point of view of the concrete existence of each of us as a free being with a project?

To begin with: the view that truth is a matter of interpretation largely coincides with the overall modern critique of the social lie that has always propped up the power of the strong over the weak. Nietzsche (yes, him again) used to say that the voice of conscience that we feel inside us is only the voice of the herd, the pressure of a social discipline that each of us assimilates and turns into a personal *daimon*. Precisely of that which appears most evident, he adds, we ought to be most mistrustful—for the same reason. Marx's critique of ideology is likewise grounded, in the last analysis, on the same constatation of the interpretive character of truth: ideology is an instance of interpretation (on the part not just of individuals but of social classes) unaware of itself, and for just that reason convinced that it is absolute truth. In general, the whole area covered by the term "school of suspicion" (another Nietzschean expression, taken up by Paul Ricoeur), which obviously includes Freudian psychoanalysis, is an array of variations on the theme of the interpretive character of every experience of truth. That's not all. Clearly the hermeneutic stance has links to deconstructionist thought inspired by Derrida and also to a great deal of postanalytic philosophy influenced by the so-called second Wittgenstein. When the latter talks about "linguistic games," within the bounds of which truth can arise only out of the observance of shared rules, never out of evidence of some correspondence with things, he is practicing hermeneutics without knowing it. As for Derridean deconstruction, it too is entirely inspired by the (highly Freudian) notion that the representation of the world in the mind is already a "second" scene springing from an earlier, more original one, and an even earlier one before that, and so on.

I take the liberty of bringing in these various currents of contemporary thought in order to situate my own discourse more firmly and to show that it is not as irrational as it might appear to be at first glance. For upon first being urged to accept that "there are no facts, only interpretations," one may feel a sudden bewilderment, a sensation of vertigo, and react in a neurotic manner, as though struck with agoraphobia, fearful of the open and indeterminate space that suddenly yawns on every side. This fearfulness may grow still more acute if one leaves the field of pure philosophy (after all, philosophers have said everything and the opposite of everything without changing the world all that much) and ventures onto the terrain of politics. Many variants of authoritarianism are revealed for what they are—claims to impose behaviors on us whether we like it or not in the name of some law of nature, human essence, sacrosanct tradition, or divine revelation—once one comes round to the view that there are no absolute truths, only interpretations. Those who tell you to "be a man" generally want to make you do something you wouldn't do willingly, like go to war or sacrifice your own interests and your legitimate (for the most part) hopes of happiness. As Wittgenstein said, philosophy frees us from idols; indeed, he was inclined to think that that was all it could do.

But liberation from metaphysically justified authoritarianism apart, dawning awareness of the interpretive character of all our experience may seem to leave one dangling in a void. Doesn't it lead down a short road to the struggle of all against all, to the pure conflict of competing interests? Or again: how would we justify, from a hermeneutic perspective, our sincere disgust at (the surfeit of) lying politicians?

If we pose these questions and try to answer them honestly (the adverb itself is not unproblematic), we will have to recognize the validity of the discourse of truth as aperture as opposed to the discourse of truth as correspondence. The latter is really only important if it serves a different truth of a higher rank. We cannot swallow the lies of Bush and Blair because they were uttered for the purpose of waging a war that we feel unable to support, that has nothing to do with us, and that violates too many of the moral principles to which we adhere. Naturally these moral principles appear "true" to us, but not in the "metaphysical" sense of the term "true," not because they correspond descriptively to some objective datum. What does it mean, for example, to oppose war because all men are brothers? Is human brotherhood really a datum to which we ought to conform because it is a fact? If you reflect on how much authority people assign, or claim to assign, to those in public life today who profess to follow scientific principles and rules, like the law of the marketplace in economics, you start to see how problematic it is to believe in an absolute duty to truth.

The whole set of relations needs to be rethought, and Machiavelli is as good a place as any to start. His error, from the vantage point of a nonmetaphysical and nonideological conception of truth at any rate, is not that he justifies lying but that he entrusts the prince alone with the right to decide when lying is justified. I daresay I would have no objection to a "democratic Machiavelli," although the expression is a contradiction in terms. Let me elaborate. Since truth is always an interpretive fact, the supreme criterion that I propose is not the close correspondence of the statement to the thing but consensus on the presuppositions that dictate how we evaluate this correspondence. No one ever tells the truth, the whole truth, and nothing but the truth. Every statement entails a choice of that which we take to be relevant, and this choice is never disinterested. Even scientists who aim in the lab to set aside private preferences, inclinations, and interests are striving for objectivity because that is the way to obtain results that can stand the test of replication and so be utilized in the future. Who knows: maybe they are only hoping to win the Nobel Prize, which is certainly a private interest.

The conclusion I wish to draw is that truth as absolute objective correspondence, as the ultimate instance and the fundamental value, is more of a danger than a blessing. It paves the way to the republic of the philosophers, the experts, the technicians, and at the limit the ethical State, which claims to be able to decide what the true good of the citizens is even in defiance of their own opinions and preferences. Wherever politics purports to seek truth, there cannot be democracy. But if truth is conceived in the hermeneutic terms proposed by many twentieth-century philosophers, truth in politics will be sought above all in the construction of consensus and civic friendship; it is these that make truth, in the descriptive sense of the term, possible. The ages when it was thought possible to ground politics in truth were ages of strong social cohesion and shared traditions but also quite often of authoritarian discipline imposed from above. An example, impressive in many respects, is the baroque age: on one hand, widespread conformism enforced by the divine right of monarchy, on the other the explicit theorization of Machiavellian reason of state. "Modern" politics, the kind handed down to us from the Europe of the Westphalian treaties, is fundamentally still like that. Even politicians involved in the swelling number of cases of official corruption, like the ones caught up in Italy's *Mani pulite* investigations, have asserted before the courts their right to lie (and steal and bribe) in the name of the public interest. They didn't steal for themselves: they did it for the party; they were making democracy work by finding innovative ways to fund it.

For a variety of reasons linked to the development of communications, the press, and the overall market for information, modern politics of that kind is no longer sustainable. The contradiction between the value of objective truth and the awareness that what we call reality is the play of interpretations in conflict has become impossible to ignore. It is impossible to win such a conflict by claiming to have found out how matters truly stand, because how they stand looks different to every player as long as there is no common horizon, no consensus about the implicit criteria on which the verification of individual propositions depends. I quite realize that this is not a solution to the problem, just a statement of it. Saint Paul uses the forceful Greek word *aletheuontes* ("truth-speaking") in his *Letter to the Ephesians* (4:15–16), which is paraphrased in the Latin Vulgate as *veritatem facientes in caritate*, literally "making truth in lovingness." At a single bound these words take us beyond the question of objectivity: what would it mean to "make truth" if truth were the correspondence of the statement to the datum? The allusion to lovingness or a loving attitude (which is what the word *caritas*, "charity," really means) is not just tacked on here. Democracy cannot dispense with the conflict of interpretations unless it is prepared to mutate into something else—the authoritarian dictatorship of experts, philosophers, savants, and central committees. But this conflict is not resolvable simply by making explicit the interests that drive the various interpretations, as though it were possible to locate a deeper truth (primal scene, infantile trauma, true Being prior to disguise) on which all could agree. The explicitation of the conflict of interpretations, the *pars destruens* of the critique of claims to absolute truth, which is the finest legacy of the school of suspicion, requires a broad horizon of civic friendliness and communitarian sharing that does not depend on the truth or falsehood of statements. That the adjective "communitarian" is bound to raise hackles is something of which I am quite well aware.

Let me repeat: this is not a solution to the problem, only a way of putting it bluntly, which at least escapes the hypocrisy of modern politics, which has never questioned the notion of truth as correspondence, while always allowing that the statesman may lie "for the good of the State" (or the party, or the class, or the homeland). This hypocrisy is deplorable not because it allows lying and so violates the absolute value of truth as correspondence but because it violates the social bond with one's fellow man. It goes, you could say, against equality and fellow feeling or against the liberty of all.

I might add that freedom is also, and primarily, the capacity to propose a truth that runs counter to common opinion. That is how Hannah Arendt takes it in her diary entries from the time of the Eichmann trial. "Truth," writes Arendt (2002, 531), "is not ascertainable through a voting procedure. Factual truth, not just rational truth, concerns man in his singularity." But in the same pages, we also find her insisting constantly that truth is always social and expressing mistrust of all who pretend to possess it in some precise and stable fashion. "Whoever, in a difference of opinion, claims to possess the truth, is attempting to establish domination" (619). This oscillation, which I think is a permanent feature of Arendt's work, is perhaps explainable by the fact that even for her truth continues to be envisaged as the objective mirroring of factual data. Despite her familiarity with existentialism, Jaspers, and indeed Heidegger, the theme of interpretation remains substantially alien to her.[3] My own preference goes to a text from the first edition of Ernst Bloch's *Spirit of Utopia* (1918), where he says that the difference between a madman and a prophet lies entirely in the capacity of the latter to found a community. I read it as another outstanding example of the transition from truth to loving charity, from the claim, always loaded with authoritarian dogmatism, that a stable foundation has been reached to the evangelical ideal of respect for the other. Of course, one needs to be able to supply arguments when engaged in social dialogue, but for the most part, they are arguments *ad homines*, appeals to our common convictions, which everyday discourse and the dominance in the media of the prevailing ideology too often forget or conceal. I have in mind things like allusions to history and the experience we share with our fellows (our group, our society, humanity itself as we perceive it in this historical moment), arguments from common sense in the loftiest sense of the term, rather than mathematical axioms and apodictic principles.

I understand that in societies that have gone through recent experiences of dictatorship and violation of human rights, as in Chile or South Africa or Nepal, the question of factual truth, the problem of finding out exactly what happened to persons who were disappeared into the vortex of police violence, is a central issue. We go through the same thing in Italy, albeit at a slightly greater distance in time, whenever someone attempts to put a gloss on the memory of fascism by denying that it was grounded in violence and the persecution of dissidents and that it actively participated in the extermination of the Jews and such other minorities as Roma, homosexuals, and handicapped persons.[4] But the drive to find out the objective truth about countless deeds of this kind would make no sense if it weren't inspired by the necessity of rendering justice, in other words prioritizing not objectivity as such but the rights of the many who suffered and still suffer and the very right of the community to remake itself into a place of shared civic life, of true political amity. The freedom of everyone has no need of truth-as-correspondence except as a means to better achieve reciprocal comprehension, that realm of the spirit in which, as Hegel put it, humanity will one day be able to feel at one with itself, "at home."

THE POLITICAL TASK OF THOUGHT

It may be helpful, in discussing the current role of philosophy in our late modern or postmodern society, to point out the analogies between a book like Popper's *The Open Society and Its Enemies* (1945) and the ideas that Heidegger expounded in numerous works, notably in a 1964 lecture entitled "The End of Philosophy and the Task of Thought." Clearly it is paradoxical to couple these two, especially since Heidegger doesn't come across as a passionately democratic thinker. Yet the reasons that drove Popper to take a stand against Plato are fundamentally the same ones that drive Heidegger in his polemic against metaphysics, which, as he writes in the opening lines of the lecture, is always Platonism, from antiquity down to Kant, Hegel, and Nietzsche. Actually, we could replace Popper's expression "open society" with the Heideggerian word *Ereignis* (event) without betraying either Popper's intentions or those of Heidegger, although neither would consent, if he were alive, to this little hermeneutical "wrench."

Popper maintains that Plato is a dangerous enemy of the open society because he has an essentialist conception of the world: all that is real responds to a law given as the structure of Being, and society too must do no more than match itself to this essential order. Since it is philosophers who know the essential order of things, to them falls the command of society. The function that philosophers—and today scientists, technicians, and experts—have assigned themselves over the centuries as the supreme advisors of princes is closely linked to the basic conviction that it is always incumbent on individuals and societies to correspond to an order of things objectively given, an order that also expresses the sole possible moral norm. Principles from the modern age such as *auctoritas, non veritas, facit legem* (authority, not truth, grounds the legal statute) have always been vulnerable to rationalistic, metaphysically inspired attack, even from the revolutionary left. Whenever truth becomes a factor in politics, the danger of authoritarianism rears its head in the shape of the "closing" that Popper stigmatizes in his writings.

Now, what Heidegger calls metaphysics is exactly the idea of Being as an order objectively given once and for all. It's the same notion that Nietzsche considered blameworthy in Socrates, whom he regarded as the initiator of the modern decadence that put an end to the tragic greatness of spirit in antiquity. If Being is a structure given once and for all, neither any aperture in history nor any liberty is thinkable.

Naturally such a vision is more reassuring than the tragic vision characteristic of the dawn of Greek thought. But this reassurance, one notes, is felt primarily by those already secure in the existing order, which they perceive on that account as rational and worthy to last for eternity; along with Nietzsche, Walter Benjamin's theses on history come to mind in this connection (1940). Early in his lecture on the end of philosophy, Heidegger (1964) adduces the name of Karl Marx, alongside that of Plato, as one who had, even earlier than Nietzsche, set about turning metaphysics (i.e., Platonism) upside down. There remains a yawning gap, of course, between Marx's upending and the "surpassing" (*Über-windung*) that Heidegger has in mind. But there is nothing arbitrary about adducing Marx's ideas on the sources of alienation in the social division of labor as an aid to understanding, with Heidegger, why and how metaphysics took such firm root in the history of our world. Here I leave to one side any discussion of the historical or eternal character of metaphysics in Heidegger's thought, which would require me to go into his dependence, never surmounted and perhaps insurmountable, on the biblical myth of original sin.

Although the notion of metaphysics is used by Heidegger in a rather idiosyncratic way, I believe that the comparison with

Popper, no matter how counterintuitive, illuminates the sense in which this notion is common to large areas of contemporary philosophy. It certainly isn't hard to discern it in Wittgenstein ("Die Welt ist alles, was der Fall ist," meaning "the world is the totality of what is the case," [Wittgenstein 1921]) and obviously in pragmatism and neopragmatism. I am well aware that the term "metaphysics" is still used, in a terminologically coherent way, by the continuators of classical thought and the neoscholastics and also by a peculiar strain of neoscholasticism that survives within analytical philosophy, in which ontology and metaphysics are used merely to indicate the structures of knowing rigidified into "regional ontologies" that have none of the elasticity and historicity that are still present in the transcendental of Kant and even Husserl. Still: it is sufficiently clear that, at any rate in large areas of contemporary philosophy, the Heideggerian notion of metaphysics as the identification of true Being with a stable structure, objectively recognizable and productive of norms, has become standard and a standard target of refutation, though the name of its principal author often goes unmentioned.

The rejection of metaphysics in this sense, whether for Nietzschean-Heideggerian reasons, or Wittgensteinian ones, or Carnapian or Popperian ones, is a good platform from which to examine the problem of the end of philosophy in the age of democracy. Indeed, going far beyond Heidegger and even Popper, we may simply identify the end of philosophy as metaphysics with the onset, political and practical, of democratic government. Where there is democracy, there cannot be a class of those who possess the true truth and either exercise power directly (Plato's philosopher-kings) or dictate rules of conduct to the sovereign. That, I repeat, is why Heidegger's reference to Marx in the lecture on the end of philosophy is telling. In the same lecture, he refers to philosophy as ending because of the dissolution it undergoes as individual sciences split off from it: from psychology to sociology, anthropology, logic, logistic systems (as they are technically called), and semantics, all the way to cybernetics (or what we would call information technology). As the reader will see, the discourse is not at all abstract, and those of us who teach philosophy in the schools and universities experience this progressive dissolution of philosophy every day. In universities that launch new courses in areas like psychology, anthropology, and the information sciences, enrollment in philosophy falls off noticeably. And so does the funding for philosophical study. Overall, this is right and inevitable, however unpleasant it may be for many of us, and especially for our students. In any case, it is a concrete aspect of the end of philosophy, and it appears to be the exclusive consequence of the increasing autonomy of the various human sciences, not a direct result of democracy. But as Heidegger also notes, it does correspond to the increasing power and social prestige of specialists and the ever-greater degree of scientific control of various aspects of community life that entails.

If you stand back and survey this panorama, you see that the end of philosophy leaves a vacuum that democratic societies cannot ignore. What I mean is, on one hand philosophy understood as the sovereign function of the wise in the government of the polis is dead and buried; on the other, as Heidegger hints in the title of his lecture, where he speaks of the "task of thought" after the end of philosophy/metaphysics, there remains the problem, specifically democratic, of keeping the unchecked power of the technicians in the various areas of social life from simply replacing the authority of the philosopher-kings. Unchecked—and dangerous, because more deceptive and more ramified, so much so that an old-fashioned revolutionary plot to strike at the heart of the State would now be an absurdity, since power is objectively distributed among the many centers devoted to the various specializations. If you wanted to use a psychiatric metaphor, you could say that society was at risk for schizophrenia, with a regime of doctors and nurses, straitjackets and restraining beds as the fallback locus of power.

So let's rewrite the title of Heidegger's lecture to read "The End of Philosophy in Democratic Societies and the (Political) Task of Thought." The sovereign role of the philosopher has come to an end, because sovereigns have come to an end. Whether or not any relation of cause and effect exists between these terminations is not easy to tell. Like Marx, Heidegger would say that the end of metaphysics and so of philosophy's claims to sovereignty is not something that was brought to pass primarily by philosophers. For him, of course, the whole matter would be in the nature of an event of Being, with the philosopher's only option being to co-respond to it. But it is plain to see that the distance from that to Marx is not enormous: where does the Being to which the philosopher must respond speak? Not in the economic and material structure of society, certainly, or not solely and exclusively there. That it is possible for me at this point to put forward an interpretive hypothesis that, albeit still relatively audacious, would have been unthinkable thirty years ago—the proposal to compare the open society of Karl Popper to the end of metaphysics in the thought of Martin Heidegger—is not the upshot of some philosophical discovery but a response, for what it is worth, to the changing times. With respect to the moment at which Popper and Heidegger were situated, the world today has gone farther down the road of integration and scientific rationalization, so that the end of philosophy, both in the sense of its dissolution into the various sciences and in the sense of the vacuum and the absence that it leaves within democracy itself, is now much more visible and pervasive. In advancing the view that there are analogies between Heidegger and Popper, I am not discovering some deeper truth; that would be another form of metaphysical thinking, with claims to absoluteness. But I am corresponding to what has come about, to the event—in the specifically Heideggerian sense of the term also.

The task of thought in this situation, whether one's references are Heidegger or Marx, perhaps not Popper, is to think that which remains hidden in the "ongoing presentation" of what is ceaselessly coming about. For Marx, that means the dialectical concreteness of the linkages that ideology conceals from us; for Heidegger, it means truth as *aletheia*, as the opening of a horizon (or a paradigm) that renders possible any truth understood as conformity to the state of things, the verification or falsification of propositions (see Heidegger 1951). Naturally, Popper will no longer be our companion as we push the discourse to this point, because the allusion to Marx or to the "hidden" that demands to be thought seems to take us a long way from the open society. It would take too long here to demonstrate that actually the comparison to Heidegger and Marx in the terms I have proposed still holds good, so let's leave Popper out of it. The pairing of Marx and Heidegger, which the latter himself suggests in the lecture under discussion, retains all its force. But is it really possible to speak about the hidden *aletheia* to which Heidegger alludes as though it were the same thing as the concreteness of socioeconomic relations in Marx? In other words: how is the task of thought configured after the end of philosophy, when philosophers no longer think they have privileged access to ideas and essences enabling them to govern or supply the governor with norms? If we were to stick exclusively with Marx, we would be going back to a rationalist and historicist metaphysics in which the philosopher's task is to express the definitive truth of history, which only the expropriated proletariat knows and which it realizes in the revolution.

Not even Marx, ultimately, knew how to really look at Being as event, which is why Popper was right to regard him as an enemy of the open society. But if we follow Heidegger exclusively, we risk entanglement in the kind of *grundlose Mystik, schlechte Mythologie, verderblicher Irrationalismus* (Heidegger 1964: "groundless mysticism, bad mythology, detrimental irrationalism") that he himself perceives to be the risk to which his own position is exposed. To neutralize this risk, which attends not just Heidegger but a good deal of today's philosophy (of the kind at any rate that refuses to become a mere appendage, more or less superfluous, of the human sciences and the sciences in general), we need to go further down the road of what Jürgen Habermas called the "urbanization of the Heideggerian backwoods" begun by Hans-Georg Gadamer. Such an urbanization requires the liberation of Heidegger from "groundless mysticism," by taking the invocation of Marx beyond his own original intentions. In the lecture on "The Origin of the Work of Art" (1936), Heidegger had included, among the modes in which truth comes about, not just art but also the whole area of religion, ethics, politics, "essential thought." These hints remained undeveloped in the later course of his thinking. But in any case it is not a question here of remaining more or less faithful to his teaching but of searching for ways to solve the problem we face, which is the task and the future of philosophy after it has ended. In the epoch of the end of metaphysics we can no longer search, as Heidegger did, for the event of Being in those privileged moments on which he himself always concentrated: the great poetic works, "inaugural" words like the saying of Anaximander or the poem of Parmenides or the lines of Hölderlin. These texts continue to function as essences, Platonic ideas recognized only by philosophers, who sometimes make them into "sovereign" voices. In the age of democracy, the event of Being to which thought must turn its attention is something much broader, perhaps, and less well defined, something more like politics. The only aid we have in thinking it is an expression from the late Foucault, which I adopt but use in an autonomous sense: "the ontology of actuality." The event (of Being) to which thought has the task of corresponding in the age of democracy is the mode in which Being is configured on an ongoing basis in the collective experience. The hidden that tends to vanish in the specialization of the sciences is *Being qua Being*, the integrality of individual and social experience that needs to be protected from technological schizophrenia and the lapse into authoritarianism that it entails. To speak here of ontology, and to entrust this task once again to philosophers no longer sovereign, no longer counselors of princes, certainly means imagining a new, as yet undefined, role for the intellectual: not a scientist, not a technician, something more like a priest or an artist—but a priest without a hierarchy, and an artist of the streets. Less fancifully, we may imagine a figure who has a lot to do with history and politics: one who does ontology inasmuch as he or she ties current experience to experience in the past, in a continuity that is the fundamental meaning of the very term *logos*, discourse, and who constructs continuity in the community as well, promoting the formation of ever new ways of understanding ourselves (another reference to Habermas: the philosopher as *Dolmetscher* or interpreter). Some may ask: does all this really have anything to do with Being? My answer: is Being supposed to be something different, more profound, more stable and concealed, than its "event"?

FROM PHENOMENOLOGY TO AN ONTOLOGY OF ACTUALITY

Following a sort of hermeneutic circle, which philosophy cannot escape in cases like this, to propose a path running from phenomenology to the ontology of actuality is already a way of setting out down this path. But the decision to engage in this trajectory is not motivated by any general theoretical reason, no logical exigency driving phenomenology to become something different from what it has commonly been as articulated by Husserl and the more orthodox followers of the school. So it is "actuality" that demands this effort of transformation.

"Ontology of actuality" is, as I mentioned, an expression from the late Foucault, who set this "historical" way of philosophizing against what he called the "analytic of truth." What he meant by the latter term, roughly speaking, was thought whose mission is to define the conditions and the content of a truth not subject to the mutation of historical conditions, the truth that, in the philosophical tradition, down to Kant at least, was always taken to be a critical instance that reason could advance against history. Since Foucault offered no further clarification of what he meant by "ontology" and "actuality," and indeed the ontology of actuality itself became historical ontology for him, I am licensed to use these terms with a certain freedom: not just "actuality" but "ontology" as well, which Foucault certainly did not intend in the sense it has acquired in many forms of neorealism and post-analytical philosophy today. For my part, I will use "ontology" in a sense I take from Heidegger, for whom it denotes the thought of Being in both senses, subjective and objective, of the genitive. This decision alone on the meaning of the term marks a profound difference between the intent that moves these pages, and that of most ontologists, who reduce ontology to a theory of objects. As for actuality, I use this term to refer to the common condition of our life at present; this is the meaning that resonates in the use of the word in all the Romance languages: *attualità*, *actualitè*, *actu-alidad*. Evidently it is a much vaguer term and harder to define. It has the same generality and lack of sharp outline of words like modernity, postmodernity, and so on. But I might add that when empiricists speak of experience, they are not using that word in a much more precise manner.

My working hypothesis is therefore that today, in our philo-sophical and historicosocial actuality, we need to move beyond phenomenology toward an ontology of actuality. I speak of today not just with an eye on problems debated in philosophy, and in-deed I claim to speak of the world in which all we philosophers also move and live. Do I slide over into sociology? I am aware of the problem, but I will justify myself with a couple of references. One is something Lukács says in his obituary of Simmel, calling his work "sociological impressionism." The other is the concrete practice of a handful of great twentieth-century philosophers, principally Adorno, Horkheimer, Benjamin, and Heidegger. The latter is an especially important example to look to as far as I am concerned, because an interest in the actual state of human existence arose in him as a consequence of that turn in his thought that marks a shift to frankly ontological meditation.

None of these philosophers ever offered an exhaustive account of what he considered the actual human condition. The term impressionism applied to Simmel by Lukács indicates a certain partiality in the account. The fact is that, for philosophers like those I have mentioned, the decision to dedicate oneself to a given problem could be inspired only by a summons they felt coming from the world, never from a motivation internal to the logic of traditional philosophical discourse.

This, as I have noted, holds good especially for Heidegger, for whom heeding the summons of the world is precisely what constitutes the interest in ontology that blossomed (though it had never been absent in him) after the turn of the 1930s. I trust it is clear, by the way, that when I say historical situation, I mean the situation at that point in the history of philosophy, or rather in some areas of philosophy—which I am, however, willing to assume the risk of taking as characteristic of the whole epoch. There are some authoritative precedents among the philosophers I have mentioned for the inevitable partiality of such an assumption, and there is Husserl too, for whom the concept of a crisis in the European sciences certainly didn't imply a complete inventory of the world of his time.

And when I speak here of going beyond phenomenology, I am not referring primarily to Husserl as the author of *The Crisis of European Sciences* (1936). I am thinking more of eidetic phenomenology and what I would call its temptation to resolve philosophy into a number of regional ontologies, which tend to neglect fundamental ontology. Today, what I call Husserl's temptation, which underlies his break with Heidegger, is presenting itself once more in a wave of new objectivism that has arisen in some areas of European philosophy and that has links to postanalytical North American thought. Under the pressure of the countless demands for a new normativity that are directed, for the most partly unduly, at philosophy, this new objectivism often seeks to ground its response on a redefinition of the beings to which the norms are supposed to apply. The notion of "person" is a good example. Recently, even a thinker like Jürgen Habermas has proposed to revive the notion of human nature in order to make it the ground for norms in bioethics. One shares his concern about what the commercialization of genetic engineering might lead to, but there is a downside to his stance that shouldn't be ignored, and that is on striking view in the approval Habermas immediately garnered from the Vatican for his efforts. From time immemorial, the Vatican has been defending the claim that ethical norms are grounded in nature, meaning essences—which were imparted directly by God the creator, you understand, no matter what Hume might suggest, and therefore may properly serve as the ground of norms. What we see today, though I don't include Habermas in this, is that efforts to ground norms on the very nature of the beings in question often take the shape of phenomenologically inspired discourse, which finds it convenient to use the word ontology in a Husserlian sense. The mechanism I see at work in a part of contemporary European thought may be described as follows. Let us put the problem of finding out what it is we are speaking of when, for example, we speak of a person. To answer this question, following the classic procedures of analytical philosophy, one adduces all the traits that, in current linguistic usage, pertain to the notion of personhood. This is not a futile job by any means, but all it does is expand on the entry you would find in any good dictionary. The lexical definition thus constructed of the term "person" is subsequently called ontology; whoever asks what personhood is receives an answer arrived at through analysis of the usage and the connotations of the term. When Husserl wrote the article on phenomenology for the *Encyclopaedia Britannica*, was he really doing anything much different from that? The distinctions he adduces between things recalled, desired, imagined, experienced in the raw, and so on are nothing more, in the last analysis, than illustrations of linguistic usage, and maybe they couldn't be anything else. For Husserl, naturally, the legitimacy of using the word ontology to talk about these distinctions flowed directly from what was, for him, the decisive revelation of phenomenology: the fact that in eidetic intuition there is given both the specific object and the *eidos*, or rather the plural *eide*, that inseparably constitute its being. From this perspective, you might even begin to wonder if fundamental ontology is still necessary at all. Or at any rate, you begin to see why philosophy might resolve into regional ontologies. It is highly probable that Husserl, prior to *Crisis* at any rate, did think that regional ontologies might really exhaust all of philosophy, and though it can't be forensically demonstrated from the correspondence between Husserl and Heidegger at the time Husserl was writing the article for the *Encyclopaedia Britannica*, it is also inherently likely that the discord between master and disciple arose precisely out of the question of fundamental ontology and what it meant. At any rate, that is how the disagreement and the break between them look in retrospect. One's mind inevitably turns to the words Husserl wrote in a famous diary entry in 1906, where he says that he could not bear to live without the hope of attaining clarity and "an inner solidity" (September 25, 1906). There is a species of religious need permeating these lines, evident as well when he speaks of "gazing on the promised land" at the end. Do the regional ontologies and the tracing of them back to the transcendental ego really satisfy this need? We might summarize the difference between Husserl and Heidegger during the years when the former was developing phenomenology and the latter was writing *Being and Time* in simple but not unfaithful terms as the encounter between a scientific and mathematical mind and an intensely religious spirit. Husserl always attributed profound ethical significance to his own work as a phenomenologist; it is not hard to interpret that as dedication to a task that is never scrutinized closely as such. As in the case of the regional ontologies, Husserl does not question the legitimacy of the traditional division of intellectual labor: the task he assigned himself was not dissimilar to that which the neo-Kantians of the time also undertook, to wit the transcendental grounding of the specific realms of experience—the distinction among which he never doubted.

The dissatisfaction we feel today at the way in which Husserl the mathematician achieves his goal of attaining inner solidity by embracing a transcendental grounding of the regional ontologies is much the same as that which Heidegger vents in regard to Jaspers, in a review from 1919 of the latter's *Psychologie der Weltanschauungen* (which only saw print in 1976; see Heidegger 1919–1921). In that review, Heidegger critiques Jaspers for having strayed from the goal stated in his introduction, which was to study the *Weltanschauungen* as a means of probing his own. Instead of carrying out this project, Jaspers limits himself, as Heidegger sees it, to assembling a panorama of a substantially aesthetic kind, by which Heidegger means purely descriptive and objective, of the various kinds of outlook on the world. Such a panoramic stance is also evoked elsewhere in the review, in a passage referring specifically to Husserl and phenomenology.

Very briefly, if we consider *Sein und Zeit*, which Heidegger had just published in 1927, the very same year in which he was debating the *Encyclopaedia Britannica* article with his master, right in its initial pages there is a statement of the essential exigency that drives fundamental ontology: to regard the problem of Being from the viewpoint of the being posing the problem. Phenomenology as sketched in Husserl's encyclopedia article has the same defect as Jaspers's book: it leaves out the being formulating it. Of course, the shift toward transcendental phenomenology that is already detectable in the article will be a decisive step on Husserl's part toward a way of going beyond the kind of pure descriptivism and objectivism that the 1919 review imputes to Jaspers. Yet to gauge the breadth of the gap between the two men, it is enough to compare the weight borne by the term *eigentlich*, "authentic," in *Sein und Zeit* with the quite different weight it bears in a few passages from Husserl's article. Fundamental ontology involves the asker fully in the question it is asking, a question I render into Italian in the form: *che cosa ne è dell'essere?* In English, it would be something like: "just how do matters stand with Being?" or "what's going on with Being?" The phenomenological gaze, on the other hand, with its panoramic objectivity, puts one in mind of the oblivion of Being alluded to in the quotation from Plato's *Sophist* that Heidegger chose as the epigraph of *Sein und Zeit*. With our retrospective knowledge of the careers of Husserl and his disciple post-1927, we can state that what both of them were still thinking through in inchoate fashion in the year of their break was the history of Being. For Husserl, the shift to the history of Being would take place, if not achieve full resolution, in the *Crisis*, where the concern to bind eidetic phenomenology to transcendental subjectivity finds its most authentic sense (here I draw upon Enzo Paci's reading of the *Crisis*) in the ideal of a restoration of European humanity, menaced as it was by the mathematization of the fields of knowledge and the domination over the world of life exerted by the exact sciences. In Heidegger, the *Eigentlichkeit* of *Sein und Zeit* will transmute into the idea of Being as *Ereignis*, that is to say as the eventuation, which Heidegger thinks of as a giving (*Gabe, Schicken*) of the historico-destinal (*geschichtlich-geschicklich*) apertures of which the history of Being is constituted. To ponder afresh the conflictual relation between Husserl and Heidegger today is obviously more than just a historiographical exercise. To me it seems that such a rethink is needed precisely in order to liberate phenomenology from the lethal embrace, if I can call it that, of the new objectivistic ontologies that have arisen out of the encounter between bad phenomenologists and bad analytics. These ontologies have the same objectivistic, panoramic, or simply metaphysical (in the Heideggerian sense of the term) limitation that Heidegger perceived in Jaspers's book and in eidetic phenomenology: they do not put into play or put at stake (to use an idiom familiar in French and Italian) the existence of the philosopher who speaks and formulates theories. In these ontologies, the Being (of the person, of the various realms of existent things) cannot fail to be immobile and ahistorical, as geometrical as the European sciences that Husserl declared to be in crisis.

Heidegger's drive to bring the philosopher doing the speaking to the forefront of theoretical discourse arises, it seems plain enough, out of his basic existentialistic orientation. By that I mean the sort of attention to the existing individual and his or her liberty, which had been the leading motif of Kierkegaard's opposition to Hegel and which Heidegger also found in Jaspers. If I am to justify the idea that phenomenology should become an ontology of actuality, the reference to existentialism is probably not enough, not if it just means Kierkegaard and Jaspers, at any rate. Paradoxically, but not all that much, existentialism understood in these terms seems still to retain motives of an "objective" type. A philosophical theory that fails to incorporate the philosopher does not faithfully mirror "reality." Now, the campaign against metaphysics that Heidegger undertakes in the wake of *Sein und Zeit* and that is clearly perceptible in 1927 in the way that book sets about "destroying the history of ontology" cannot have motives of an even remotely objectivist kind. What does drive it, and what is detectable in the autobiographical statements made in the speech to the Heidelberg Academy for example, is what we may call the spirit of the artistic and cultural avant-garde of the early twentieth century as expounded in exemplary fashion in Ernst Bloch's *Geist der Utopie*: what you could call the spirit of expressionism, in short. A way must be found past, or beyond, metaphysics, or at any rate metaphysics must be rejected, not because it fails to include the subject of the theory and is thus incomplete but because it legitimates, with its objectivism, a social and historical order from which the liberty and originality of human existence have been erased. In *Sein und Zeit*, the idea of truth as correspondence to the datum has already been left far behind, left in the distance, so to speak, rather than being challenged for failing in turn to mirror the true (objective) essence of truth. The only motive that we can reasonably ascribe for Heidegger's antimetaphysical campaign is a practical-political one, which in Heidegger himself will only become clear over the long course of his *Kehre* (turn) but which we are now in a position to recognize with clarity. Thought that seeks a way of escape from the situation in which Being has receded into oblivion and in which objectivized beings occupy the foreground can be of only one kind: the kind that engages and involves the being that is striving to accomplish this operation above all else. Thought of that kind must perforce be an ontology of actuality—though Heidegger himself never used that expression. Here I wish to mention a great interpreter of Heidegger, Reiner Schürmann, who chose to call his fundamental study of Heidegger *Le principe d'anarchie* (1982). I advert merely to the general sense of Schürmann's work, to which I feel close primarily on account of his insistence on the problem of action. There is no possibility of exiting from metaphysics except through struggle against the fixed objectivity of the existent thing; not even *Verwindung*, for Heidegger the unique way, avails. The word "anarchy" is prominent in Schürmann, and I borrow it from him without necessarily adopting his entire theory.

The only way to try to remember Being in its difference from beings is to suspend the claim to validity of the order of beings as it is given, in fact, in our historical condition. So it becomes a matter of both attempting to descry the specific traits of the historical aperture into which we are thrown (or the Kuhnian paradigm, which allows us to speak and verify/falsify our judgments) while at the same time acknowledging its radical contingency and historicity, through a sort of self-distancing that for Heidegger is perhaps the true meaning of the phenomenological *epoché*. For that matter, this is what Heidegger says about the hermeneutic circle: it is necessary to stand inside it knowingly, not allowing chance or common opinion to impose *Vorhabe, Vorsicht, und Vorgriff* (project, foresight, and anticipation) on us (Heidegger 1927).

This passage from *Sein und Zeit* was attended by a few difficulties, because it was far from clear to the reader what it might mean to stand within the circle without yielding to current opinion yet without pretending to be able to step outside it through an "objective" vision of the thing to be known. Light can be shed on the problem, it seems to me, if we focus on the twofold significance of the ontology of actuality: making oneself aware of the paradigm into which one has been thrown yet suspending its claim to definitive validity and heeding Being as that which remains unsaid.

It is not hard to show why such thought of Being answers more adequately to the exigency driving Heidegger in his critique of Jaspers (and implicitly of Husserl too): Being comes about and is concealed in the effective historical aperture, the paradigm. Think it that way and you open yourself to Being as different from beings, Being that "anarchically" suspends the claim to definitiveness of the aperture.

With what result, one may ask. Here I feel obliged to dissent from Schürmann, at any rate if I have understood him correctly, since he, mindful of his own reading of Meister Eckhart, tends toward a species of mystical conclusion, which risks making the *epoché* into a state of total detachment from history. I myself tend to think that the heeding of Being, in the two forms I have indicated—cognizance of the paradigm and suspension of its validity through heeding the unsaid—may be specified in the following terms. The comprehension of the paradigm is nothing, fundamentally, other than the effort to comprehend dialectically the social totality into which one is thrown; Marx's historical materialism is and always will be a prime example of such an effort. And the heeding of Being as the unsaid is attention to the continually silenced voice of history's losers, those of whom Benjamin spoke. If not Heidegger himself, then certainly Schürmann would agree, I take it, with this somewhat extreme interpretation of his "principle of anarchy."

THE TARSKI PRINCIPLE

Richard Rorty wasn't exaggerating when, in his discussion with Pascal Engel on the uses of truth, he stated that he took little interest in the debate between realism and antirealism that still engages part of contemporary philosophy (see 32ff. in the English translation of Engel and Rorty 2005)—the debate on the significance of Tarski's famous principle that "P" is true if and only if P; for example "it is raining" is true if and only if it is raining. The quotation marks are decisive, obviously, or maybe not so obviously outside the circle of those interested in the debate. Indeed, to the profane, as well as to many philosophers (Rorty wasn't alone), Tarski's principle may look like one more proof that a certain style of philosophy isn't of much use anymore.

Even when reading a lucid book like *Per la verità* (*For the Truth*, but also *In Truth*) by a philosopher of unquestioned seriousness like Diego Marconi (see especially 172ff.), one cannot help feeling a certain lassitude, and at bottom the question on which the Rorty-Engel debate turned just won't go away: what's the use? But aside from the question of the utility of the debate, Marconi's book poses an even more radical problem: does that second P really lie outside quotation marks? Who says so? To face that question is to evoke the outline of Rorty's answer. Marconi maintains that whoever states that P stands outside the quotation marks is someone in whose interest it is to have that stated.

Is it possible that the second P eludes any quotation mark at all? Or at least, why stipulate at the outset that it makes no sense to pose the question? When you get right down to it, the only reason Marconi adduces for excluding the second P from quotation marks is that otherwise a large part of our discourse on the true and the false, on justified or unjustified assertions, on the rationality or irrationality of our behavior and our political and ethical decisions, would be in vain—would have no meaning. Every time we oppose a thesis or affirm one thing against something else, we are using the distinction between "P" and P. So the argument in favor of Tarski's principle is that we require it. But once again: who does? Such an argument, set against the pragmatistic "relativism" of Rorty, is clearly in self-contradiction. The Tarski thesis ought to be accepted exclusively because true, not because dictated by or to a specific audience, the notional "we" of common experience to whom Marconi also appeals to prove its validity.

As any reader who has persevered thus far will see, we get tangled up in a series of questions about which all one can say is that they don't resolve anything. Or that they can only be got round by refraining from asking "who says so?" As I see it, though, this question will not vanish unless we are prepared to make it do so by authoritative fiat—a highly unphilosophical procedure.

The question, as the reader will see, is the one that Nietzsche answered with brutal trenchancy when he wrote that "there are no facts, only interpretations. And this too is an interpretation." Even Marconi recommends accepting Tarski's thesis because we cannot do without it in accounting for our common experience. But our common experience, which Marconi often calls the maximum of evidentness available here and now, is an interpretation. We tend to avoid calling it that solely in order to distinguish it from more markedly individual opinions, which we dismiss as "just" interpretations. Even the history of the universe before we came along is something we can only talk about inasmuch as one way or another we "feel" its effects.

Does defending the interpretive character of any assertion about the facts amount to maintaining that things are not unless we invent them (empirical idealism)? Or that the order in which they appear to us is an order that we ourselves establish, more or less arbitrarily (a subjectivistic-transcendental idealism of sorts)? Kant, who isn't exactly a nobody, maintained that about things in themselves we know only that which we receive as phenomena within the format of our a priori (time, space, the categories of the intellect). And he added that this was not a warrant to cancel any distinction between chatter and "true" statements. If I say that the difference between true and false is always a difference between interpretations more acceptable and shared and those less so, I am maintaining the same distinction, and I have no need to imagine a fact that "there is" beyond any human reach.

Who is left unsatisfied by this solution? What or whom does "truth" without quotation marks serve? Maybe, as Marconi suggests, it serves to raise questions about the existing order—enlightenment and revolution, human rights versus totalitarianism, advances in knowledge versus obscurantism? Totò, the famous Italian comedian, would have said: "Ma ci facciano il piacere." In modern English idiom, we would say: "Oh, give us a break." Who was it that always thundered against Kant and his perverse subjectivism? It was the Catholic Church, and often monarchs and governments too. Of course that "proves" nothing from the viewpoint of a Tarskian. Let's just take it as a warning to pay attention.

And to discover a "truth" about truth? To affirm that "it is true" that the Tarski thesis helps those in power impose their own interpretation as the only true one? No, we stop short of that. As good pragmatists, with maybe a tincture of Marxist critique of ideology, all we will affirm is that this is what sounds true "to us," what is able to set us free. We can never claim that our point of view is the same as God's. We can only acknowledge that we see things on the basis of certain prejudices, certain interests, and if truth is possible at all, it is the result of an accord that is not necessitated by any definitive evidence, only by loving charity, solidarity, the human (all-too-human?) need to live in harmony with others. Does positing all this—that loving one's neighbor is a duty, that solidarity is better than struggle—signify that we believe it because it is a fact, like a P without quotation marks? Perhaps not even Tarski in person would maintain that.

PHILOSOPHY AND POLITICS

I pose the problem of the relation between philosophy and politics at a time characterized, in my view, by two events that I am prepared to run the risk of calling "epochal."[5] On one hand, philosophy has lived and is still living through a process that Heidegger called "the end of metaphysics," the crumbling of the claims of foundational thought and the consequent "crisis of reason," which is a circumstance hard to ignore, although as a slogan it may have been oversold a bit. On the other—political—hand, the collapse of real socialism has cast a pall of general discredit over political ideologies of the "deductive" and overarching type and promoted the expansion of a "Popperian" style of liberalism that limits itself to thinking politics in terms of small steps, of trial and error, of extreme pragmatic concreteness. And these two events are interrelated, there is no doubt, though not by any causal dependency. Indeed, long before real socialism collapsed, the political and cultural underpinning needed for universalistic thought of any kind had buckled, with the end of colonialism, the cultural and political self-assertion of peoples round the world, the widespread impact of cultural anthropology, and the shattering in the 1914–1918 war of the myth of unilinear human progress led by the civilized West. And along with all that had gone the crisis of metaphysics (in the Heideggerian sense).

So if that is a broadly adequate sketch of the overall situation, a sort of "prologue in heaven" to the main action, what we have before us in the here and now is a scene of political parties in crisis, some destroyed by endemic corruption, of course, but all of them sapped of their vitality by the enslavement of much of their traditional "public" to the electronic media. And that has drastically changed the relation of the philosopher to politics. The organic intellectual lost his role and his legitimacy with the end of Marxist communism, which by the way I see not as having been defeated but simply as having run its course. But apart from that, he has no one to address in the way that he could once address a political party. The only recourse for the intellectual is to address public opinion in general, but you can hardly call that a real political role. If he comments on current affairs and publishes opinion pieces, then he is more than just a specialist or technician, and he has the traits of the intellectual in the Gramscian sense of the word, but he is really operating much like anyone else who writes for a living, or even like a creative artist, anyone whose relation to political and social reality is mediated by the mechanism of the (free and neutral?) market.

This may look like a marginal and exclusively practical aspect of the problem, but it isn't. The philosopher's relation to politics is certainly a matter of content, of what he has to say to the politician, more than anything else. But this content is profoundly marked by the setting in which it is elaborated and expressed. Until a few years ago at any rate, philosophy in Italy had noticeably greater public presence in the media than was the case, for example, in the English-speaking world, and that cannot be unrelated to the fact that, ever since the Gentile reform in 1923, philosophy has been taught as a regular curriculum subject in a large part of the secondary-school system. I mention this only to make the point that, in discussing philosophy and politics, one needs to pay attention to how those who profess philosophy in our societies actually live and especially to the place of philosophy as a school subject (which I believe ought to be larger than it is).

The two macroevents with which I began make the relation of philosophy to politics more difficult, but they also create possibilities. The parallel and connected dissolution of metaphysics and real socialism have brought to an end the age of the philosopher as adviser of princes, whether it was an eighteenth-century *philosophe* counseling an enlightened monarch or an organic intellectual counseling Gramsci's new prince, the political party. Those who formulate government policy in industrialized societies sometimes seem to think that, since we have ascended to the positive stage, the philosopher's place has been taken by the scientist and the economist and their ilk. But if that were a valid way of looking at things, which it isn't, the traditional, "metaphysical" (and authoritarian) relation of philosophy to politics would still be intact, except that one type of scientist, obsolete because unspecialized, would have been replaced by another. There is, though, an authentic parallel in politics to the end of metaphysics: the rise of democracy. Philosophy for its part discovers that reality cannot be captured in a system that is logically compact and that yields conclusions applicable to political decision making. Politics for its part experiences its own incapacity to conform to truth, since it has to let itself be driven by the play of majorities and minorities and the democratic consensus. This divorce of politics from truth is a point worth making, for those of us in Italy and the Catholic world anyway, perpetually solicited as we are to adapt the laws of the State to fit what the Church considers to be metaphysical truth regarding human nature, the good, and justice.

Naturally a politics without truth need not be solely and necessarily a democratic politics; it might also be a despotic politics that, instead of moving beyond metaphysics, simply refuses to recognize or respond to the natural rights of man (itself a piece of metaphysics, granted). It seems to me that concerns like these, along with awareness of the utter impossibility of grounding a rational politics in philosophy, are the source of those political philosophies that concentrate on the philosophical legitimation of democracy and more generally of the liberal State (see, for example, Habermas 1992). I will not tarry here over the question of whether positions like those of Habermas and Apel, which I would call transcendental proceduralism, have the capacity to develop beyond the legitimation of democracy, in the direction of substantive choices in favor of this or that politics, of this or that particular model of State and society. Whatever the answer to that may turn out to be, it is sufficiently clear that such positions remain within a model that we can call traditional, or in my terms, metaphysical, of the philosophy-politics relationship: the necessity or the duty to construct democratic societies derives from a philosophical reflection on the conditions of possibility of any reasoned discourse—on penalty, ultimately, of the performative contradiction that serves as Apel's *passe-partout* but that also undergirds the Habermasian theory of communicative action. It hardly needs to be said that I find nothing to object to in the political conclusions at which Apel and Habermas arrive by different routes. It does appear to me, though, that their discourse exudes a certain air of political futility, by which I mean only that they still remain within the ivory tower of academic specialization at a time when the legitimacy of liberal democracy is practically no longer contested by anyone. Apel and Habermas seem unable to really come to terms with the altered circumstances not just of political philosophy but of philosophy period, upon which it seems to me that democracy has forced far deeper changes than a discourse of legitimation conducted from an essentialist or in any case transcendental point of view can adequately address.

Whether it presents itself as a theory legitimating a certain form of State or aims to promote more substantive and specific political choices, philosophy today can no longer speak from a foundational point of view. If it does adopt, even only implicitly, such a point of view, it exposes itself to the consequence of having to make its own efficacy depend on an alliance with a prince, ancient or modern, meaning on some form of authoritarianism. Consider, if you will, the Habermasian and Apelian notion of unhindered social communication. It provokes the persistent suspicion that the electorate is being manipulated by the elite through the mass media and that therefore the verdict of the ballot box is always to some greater or less extent vitiated because not truly free. Such suspicion might serve as a guideline for the drafting of legislation to protect freedom of the press or to break up information monopolies. But if you think it right through, it always takes for granted the link between politics and truth and thus risks having to accept some form of mandarinate entrusted with the task of invigilating the transparency of communication.

So it seems to me that, while it remains important to consider the specific circumstances attending the relation of philosophy to politics today (the media society, the problem of philosophy as a school subject, the fading away of the parties), the principal question we ought to be trying to answer is: what becomes of the philosophy-politics relation in a world in which, in consequence of the end of metaphysics and the spread of democracy, politics can no longer be thought in terms of truth? The double condition of difficulty and opportunity in which philosophy finds itself in this environment consists of the fact that, on the one hand, it can no longer supply politics with guidance derived from its knowledge of essences, foundations, or even the conditions of possibility, and on the other, since it neither can nor should any longer be foundational thought, philosophy becomes intrinsically political thought, in the form of what I have proposed to call the ontology of actuality. In brief, it is conceived as the (most persuasive) response to the Heideggerian summons to recover the memory of Being. This appeal was not formulated (in *Sein und Zeit*) in the name of an abstract need for cognoscitive completeness (a fundamental ontology is required to ground the regional ontologies—Husserl's point of departure in *Die Krisis*) but in reaction to the fragmentation of experience and of the very notion of reality that is produced in modernity. "Weberian" modernity, characterized by specialization, the separation of the spheres of existence and value, and the multiplication of sectoral languages, is where the memory of what Being signifies gets lost. However, since the outcome of Heidegger's reflection leads to the recognition that "there is not" Being but that it befalls, and so we are unable to return to, or recover knowledge of, an object given in presence once the mist of forgetting into which it has slipped is dispelled, the re-memoration of Being will signify, provided we are willing to interpret Heidegger even against the grain of certain self-misunderstandings on his part, the effort to understand what "Being" means in our actual experience.

On that base, I see nothing scandalous in maintaining that a "re-memorating" (*andenkend*) thought, as Heidegger thinks that a non- or postmetaphysical thought must be, may also be qualified as democratic thought. What it heeds in its effort of re-memoration is not just the voice of an archaic original mystery supposedly lost in the precipitous onset of modernity; there is no origin placed somewhere outside the actuality of the event. There is the density of the event, which certainly bears the imprint of the past but which is equally composed of the voices of the present, and the past itself is something to which we accede only through whatever part of it survives down to us, its *Wirkungsgeschichte*.

Can philosophy that has let go of the illusion of foundation really continue to call itself ontology? Some interpreters and radical continuators of Heidegger, Derrida first and foremost, deny that one can still speak of Being, because that would be a form of relapse into the metaphysics of foundation. Yet still to speak of Being and ontology is not an overweening stance; indeed, it is an expression of modesty on the part of this philosophy: free of the obligation to respond to truth, it need only respond to the need for the recomposition of experience for a historical humanity that is living through the fragmentation of the division of labor, the specialization of languages, the multiple forms of discontinuity to which the rapidity of the transformations, primarily technological, of our world are exposing us. To turn away from Being is only possible, vice versa, if one neglects this modest task and assumes the age-old burden of responding to an objective truth about things that excludes such a fiction as being at once too vague and too rigid. When defined as the ontology of actuality, philosophy is practiced as an interpretation of the epoch that gives form to pervasive sentiments about the meaning of actual existence (in other words, existence now), in a certain society and in a certain historical world. I realize that rediscovering philosophy as the spirit of the times, à la Hegel, sounds like announcing the invention of the wheel. The difference lies in the word "interpretation": philosophy is not the expression of the epoch; it is an interpretation that naturally strives to be persuasive but that acknowledges its own contingency, liberty, riskiness. Not only does Hegel appear to reemerge; empiricism too has a role: the epoch, and the pervasive sentiments about what it means, might just be another word for experience, to which empiricism strove to be faithful—experience philosophically interpreted, using the instruments handed down to us by a certain textual tradition, out of which certain elements, aspects, and authors are foregrounded in preference to others but that remains available as the background in its totality, as the possible source of alternative interpretations.

However this proposal is assessed, it is clear at least that it configures an alternative to the philosophies that are still claiming for themselves a foundational function with respect to politics (or even just the transcendental legitimation of a certain form of government, whatever may be the specific choices that are made following those rules of the game). Abandoning any foundational pretense, an ontology of actuality offers politics a certain vision of the historical process under way[6] and a certain free and risk-laden interpretation of its positive virtualities, judged to be such not on the basis of eternal principles but on the basis of choices argued for within the process itself (when we are on a path, we already know more or less where we are headed). Rorty used to speak of a Kantian lineage and a Hegelian lineage running through today's thought. Well, here we are obviously in the Hegelian lineage, in the sense that philosophy makes a commitment vis-à-vis history, bets on certain outcomes rather than others, and so abandons its position of transcendental neutrality—a position to which remain linked not just the explicit reprises of Kantianism (the case of Apel and Habermas) but also much of analytically inspired political thought.

The ontology of actuality, when the time comes to go beyond programmatic statements to concrete elaborations, doesn't have an easier time of it than the foundational philosophies. If anything, the work turns out to be more arduous because, to revert to one of my initial remarks, the socioprofessional condition of its practice is still mainly cut to the figure of the traditional philosopher, or at most that of the scientist, the specialist, the academic with a mission to excavate rigorously one small corner of the vast world of knowledge. On top of that, with the political parties crumbling like sand castles and political associationism in general withering away, any possibility of supplementary social support for the philosopher has practically vanished. Hence the difficulties entailed by the philosopher's effort to give form to pervasive sentiments, to democratically "represent" in some measure the actual sense of Being, are almost insurmountable.

The distance between philosophy and its times, even in this form, which ought in principle to be more open to dialogue with politics, remains huge. But reflection on philosophy and politics, even if (from my point of view) it doesn't get us very far toward renewing the relation and the contribution of philosophy to politics, may at least succeed in summoning philosophy to a more radical awareness of what the event, if that is what it is, of the end of metaphysics and the advent of democracy in thought signifies.

ONLY A RELATIVISTIC GOD CAN SAVE US

What Heidegger said in his throwaway remark to *Der Spiegel* was "nur noch ein Gott kann uns retten," which is usually rendered in English as "only a God can still save us." To adapt it to read "nur noch ein relativistischer Gott kann uns retten," as my subtitle suggests, is more than just a provocative piece of wordplay. Heidegger himself might not have disowned it, had he lived to see the damage being done in our time by religious fundamentalism, real or phony (for I don't in the least suppose that Bush and his cronies are true believers). To make it a bit less provocative, we could change "relativistic" to "kenotic," matching more closely the image of God available to us as Christians today.

Even the word *noch* I regard as essential. In German it implies "at the point we've reached now" or "at this point." A relativistic or kenotic God is what is given to us today, at this point in the history of salvation, and thus also at this point in the history of the Church, Catholic or generically Christian, in the world of realized globalization. I emphasize the connection with the here and now, because for us as for Heidegger, the God that could save us is not a metaphysical entity objectively given, the same for eternity, that we need only "discover" through some sort of

Cartesian meditation capable of demonstrating to us his indubitable existence.

Nobody ever really starts from zero, and a God of that kind is virtually meaningless from within the (Heideggerian) perspective of the end of metaphysics. I pose the problem of God, of what this noun signifies for us, within a determinate historical condition; even those who don't live the life of a Church or have religious experience of any kind still face the aftermath of the problem of God as it was posed in the religions that historically existed and in the Christian West that was the Church. Heidegger implies as much in a course he taught in the academic year 1919–1920, *Introduction to the Phenomenology of Religion*. In it he moves from general notions about religion in the first part to a commentary on one of the Pauline letters in the second part, without even bothering to explain why (Heidegger 1920–1921b). Having demonstrated at length in the first part that one can only speak of religion out of a concrete existential experience of it, he will not have felt the need to account for narrowing in on Saint Paul, because he will have assumed that he and his hearers of that era had all had experience of that kind. If anything, what does stand out in hindsight is the persistence of a few prejudices arising out of phenomenology, especially the idea that in order to speak of the Christian experience it is necessary to backtrack to some original, generative moment. What does the example of Heidegger, what does all that we have learned from him, mean for us today? Just that we are compelled to pose the problem of God at this particular moment in salvation history in relation to our experience of the Church and Christianity in the here and now.

Now, our daily experience of salvation history is greatly affected by fundamentalism—and I am quite well aware of the problem in saying "we," but it is either that or discourse of a purely intimistic and solipsistic kind, however empirical it might pretend to be. There is the fundamentalism of the so-called Islamic terrorists, who are, to a large extent anyway, just rebels fighting against Western domination, which the West keeps ratcheting up the more threatened it feels. But above all there is the fundamentalism that bulks larger and larger in Western religion itself, perhaps in part as a reaction against the liberation struggles of the formerly colonial peoples. I don't think this is just an Italian particularity. Phenomena of secularization have grown increasingly frequent everywhere, and the Church seems to react the same way everywhere. We here in Italy can certainly testify that the Catholic Church never stops pressing its agenda to have its authority recognized, the rationale being that the Christian revelation empowers it to defend the authentic "nature" of mankind and civil institutions. Christian thought may struggle to remain current, and even the Catholic hierarchy may strive to read the signs of the times and speak to those living in the present. But there is no doubt that, deep down, it sees modernity as the enemy. Countless pontifical pronouncements about these problems confirm it. There is the battle being waged—and still undecided as I write—by the ecclesiastical hierarchy to have the Christian roots of our civilization mentioned explicitly in the European Constitution. There is the recent opposition to any legislation that gives an inch on topical issues in bioethics like genetic engineering, assisted pregnancy, euthanasia, or homosexual families. There are the priestly thunderbolts directed from papal and episcopal sees at the perils of "relativism," by which they really mean the liberal society we are living in. All these are symptoms, telling us that the Church finds the modern world, with its prevalent laicity, a harsh environment. For the Church, the ideal society remains one in which God is the foundation of human coexistence and where the Church's claim to speak on his behalf goes unchallenged. Not only is this last profession incompatible with a multicultural society that is by definition egalitarian and neutral with respect to the ethical variations between one culture and another, but the very notion of a God "grounding" the human world, though the matter might not be put in such bluntly metaphysical terms, clashes frontally with a culture that largely rejects the very notion of foundation or ground, at any rate when the problem is posed in sufficiently explicit terms. What immediately comes to mind is that phrase from the late Heidegger about "letting go of Being as ground."[1] But this goes beyond Heideggerianism. Here we see the Church rejecting a huge area of contemporary philosophy in the name of a monotheistic metaphysics, which it maintains is inseparable from Christianity and therefore the only possible portal to salvation.

Aggiornamenti on the Church's part come and go, yet it is no exaggeration to say that they are still where they were when they put Galileo on secret trial. They may have given up attempting to make the Bible account for the cosmos and the laws of motion of the heavenly bodies, but they still prate about a "biblical anthropology" to which the laws of the State must conform if human nature is not to be violated. That is why they fight so hard against divorce, abortion, and homosexual unions and why genetic engineering, even for therapeutic ends, horrifies them so much. (Habermas and the pope seem to be converging on issues like these.) Another proof of the fact that the Church hasn't really got past the stage of the Galileo trial is that those who are abandoning Christianity are doing so for reasons that boil down to the ecclesiastical claim to know what the true nature of man, the world, and society is. That is the source of the unending debate about creationism and anticreationism, which is an analogue of the Galileo trial. It's the same old story of their wanting to affirm that the God of Jesus is the maker of the material world and thus the source of its regulatory laws, a sort of supreme clockmaker who always needs a theodicy because, strictly speaking, miracles ought to be beyond his power and because he owes us an explanation for all the ills he permits. In this respect, the reflections of Jewish theologians after Auschwitz have something to teach their Christian counterparts: not only can God not be omnipresent and good at the same time, but it may no longer be possible to think of him as the Platonic demiurge, as the producer of the material world and thus answerable for the sometimes dreadful way it functions. Today the defense of creationism, even in the face of the (adequately) proven Darwinian theory of evolution, acts as a barrier, a *pietra di scandalo* or "pebble of scandal," as we say in Italian, to the acceptance of Christianity. But it's the same pebble on which many believers stumble when they find themselves rationally unable to accept the sexual and family ethics preached by the pope, just as they found totally unacceptable John Paul II's repeated prohibition on the use of condoms, in disdain of the potentially lethal effects such a ban might have, and may indeed have had, on a world ravaged by AIDS. What keeps on recurring is the "scandal," in one form or another, of Christian preaching claiming to dictate the "truth" about how matters "really stand" with nature, mankind, society, and the family: God is the foundation, and he speaks through the Church, which has been authorized by him to decide in the last instance.

Not to face up to these difficulties or to the scandal that the Church's teaching provokes in those trying to believe in Jesus Christ—never mind the immorality on the part of the priesthood and the hierarchy that so frequently makes the headlines—is to retreat into fundamentalism. Whether this holds good everywhere and always I do not know, but it seems obvious to me that today the Church's true vocation should be to escape from fundamentalism. Its resistance to modernity is reaching such extremes that it will inevitably lead to a backlash. Even believers who do not feel doubt and do accept the preaching and the discipline succeed in doing so only by setting brackets in their minds around these brazenly reactionary attitudes. Today only a tiny fraction of self-described practicing Catholics, ones who take the sacraments assiduously, say that they accept and try at least to practice the sexual ethics promoted by the pope.[2] They just don't take it seriously, any more so than the hordes of young people who turn up at his rallies but certainly use condoms in their sexual relations. If this is, as I take it to be, a faithful portrait of the situation, then it would seem that the effort of the Church hierarchy to combat secularization by adopting a stricter code of discipline is having a paradoxical effect, tending to create an attitude of weary resignation among the faithful, who don't break with the hierarchy only because they aren't really listening any more. One recalls all that has been said over the ages about the flexible manner in which the Catholics of southern Europe believe and practice their religion. Mediterranean Catholicism has always been regarded as a form of religiosity less serious than that which drove Protestantism and caused the wars of religion in early modern Europe. In the north, the mass and the prayer book were translated into the living tongues so that the faithful would make a firmer commitment to their doctrinal content; in the south, Christianity was professed as pure and simple membership in a common and unquestioned culture. Today, faced with the harm that fundamentalism is doing in the Christian world, for example by reigniting the dispute between science and belief or between Church and State on matters of civil legislation (as in the bioethical domain), we may well think that the flexible religiosity of traditional Catholicism has a lot to be said for it. If the Church continues to think of faith as a deposit of truths more certain than those ascertained by science, continues to profess a more or less literal creationism, and continues to try to impose its own biblical anthropology on the State, it is fated to dwindle away, in a world where science and human rights are becoming universal.

To speak of a "kenotic" or relativistic God is to fully accept that the age of the Bible as a deposit of knowledge, the truth of which is guaranteed by divine authority, is over and gone, and that this is not an evil to which Christianity must temporarily adapt while waiting for the moment of revanche but is part of salvation history. Gustavo Bontadini, a great Italian Catholic philosopher who taught for many years at the Catholic University of Milan, used to say that when the Church feels weak it talks about freedom, and when it feels strong it talks about truth. The insistence, even in the encyclical *Deus caritas est*, on the inseparability of charity from truth is a sign that the Church continues to long for its former position of strength, from which it could impose the truth that it believes that God has handed down to it. But is the world now, and in the foreseeable future, really ready to acknowledge Catholic truth and give the Church of Rome back its "strength"? Today there are signs that the major religions are drawing closer to one another. But to the extent that is the case, it certainly isn't happening in the areas of dogma and doctrine. Are we Christians really supposed to think that humanity will be saved only when all men believe that God is three persons and one at the same time and that the Virgin Mary was raised up bodily into heaven? I am not recommending that the pope be more "realistic" and less intransigent with the other religions so as to edge them closer to acceptance of the message of Jesus. It seems to me that the stripping away from the gospel message of all that keeps it at a distance from the men and women of the various cultures who are encountering and confronting one another in our time is a new phase in the history of Christian salvation. It is the incarnation understood as *kenosis* that is being realized more fully today, as Christian doctrine sheds the elements of superstition that have characterized it in the distant and recent past. And of these superstitions the most grave and dangerous is the belief that faith is objective "knowledge" of God (did he really intend to reveal to us what his "nature" is like?) and the laws of creation, from which all the norms of individual and collective life derive. Superstition of that kind may be no more than an innocent attachment to outdated ideas, but it is far more likely to spring from a tendency to authoritarianism that has never disappeared from the Church's tradition. It is the claim to exert command in the name of the nature of the world and mankind that enables the Church to attempt to impose its own principles even on nonbelievers, in opposition to the principles of laicity, tolerance, and even charity.

Even if one looks at the world situation in general, not just the history of Christianity, the idea of *kenosis*, which for Christians is the very meaning of the incarnation and is thus at the center of the history of salvation, is ineluctable from the point of view of the destiny of metaphysics. The dissolution of the reasons for fundamentalism is a general fact; in Heidegger's theory, metaphysics is destined to finish at the moment at which its domination culminates. This thesis is broadly similar to that of Adorno, in which the "truth" of Hegelianism, in which "totality is the truth," is upended or reversed into its contrary at the moment when the "totalization" of the real becomes a fact. Likewise metaphysics for Heidegger culminates and finishes in the world of *Ge-Stell*, of the total organization realized in late capitalism and in the triumph of quantifying rationality. At this point it becomes impossible to think Being as objective rationality, because, thought in that way, it would just be the ground of the dehumanization of the world, where all that exists is functionality predetermined by a colossal mindless mechanism.

Seen in this light, the *kenosis* that is the original meaning of Christianity signifies that salvation lies above all in breaking the identification of God with the order of the real world, in distinguishing God from (metaphysical) Being understood as objectivity, necessary rationality, foundation. Even to think of God as the creator of the material world is to subscribe to this metaphysical conception of the divine, which today has come to an impasse precisely on account of the totalitarianism being realized all around us in the disciplined society of economic integration and pervasive monitoring employing the latest information technology. A God "different" from metaphysical Being can no longer be the God of definitive and absolute truth that allows no doctrinal variation. That is why he may be called a "relativistic" God. A "weak" God, if you will, who does not show us our weakness as a way of asserting (against rational expectation, as a mystery to which we must submit, as the ecclesiastical discipline we must accept) that he is luminous, omnipotent, sovereign, and awesome, that he bears all the traits of the threatening and reassuring personage of natural-metaphysical religiosity. Christians are called to experience God differently than that in the world of the explicit multiplicity of cultures; the alternative of claiming to think the divine as absoluteness and "truth" in violation of the precept of charity is no longer an option.

NIHILISM, SEXUALITY, POSTMODERN CHRISTIANITY

Belief in the importance of sexuality in human life is gradually waning. Those who are still clinging to it are psychoanalysts and the clergy (in the generic sense, not just the Catholic priesthood). That pairing might seem counterintuitive, but it has literal validity to the extent that these two groups of "believers in sex" are in fact representatives of social authority and the imperative norm of an order still largely based on the Oedipal rule, which governs the reproduction of social life and the self-perpetuation of society. The power of this social normality depends on the lack of an alternative model of the family, of education, of the theory and practice of authority. Conservatives assert that this lack is actually proof that the "Oedipal" order is the only natural one. We in Italy are faced every day with the "naturalism" of the Catholic Church, but I don't imagine that in the United States, never mind the Islamic world, things are very different. The Catholic Church's campaign in Italy against legislative proposals to confer legitimacy on the "civil partnerships" of unmarried couples, gay or straight, is based on the conviction that the family is "naturally" heterosexual. The State is therefore barred from recognizing any right to form unions that diverge from that natural model:

otherwise it would be furthering the dissolution of the basis of the whole social order, which is protected exclusively by the monogamous, heterosexual, reproductive, and (if possible) indissoluble union that is the traditional family in the Christian West. The key point in the Church's obstinate persistence in emphasizing homosexuality as the worst of perversions is not, as one might be tempted to think, a matter of internal discipline, given all the scandals involving pedophile Catholic priests that have come to light in recent years and the problems that obviously arise in all-male institutions like seminaries. The point is that the Church is fully aware that its hard-line stance to the effect that only reproductive sexuality is legitimate is the cornerstone of its claim to stand for the "natural" order handed down by the Creator himself. Original sin disrupted it, but then Jesus came to restore it by giving the Church the means of salvation: the sacraments it administers and the truth it teaches. The Church's battle against homosexual "marriage" is actually many battles in one; fundamentally it sees the "nature" of the human being under threat from biotechnology and genetic engineering, and there is a good deal of validity in that stance. On this matter an unexpected ally has recently rallied to the Church's side, in the person of Jürgen Habermas, with his talk about "human nature." This is rather surprising coming from a philosopher who has hitherto had a humanistic-historicist, and consequently Hegelian-Marxist, vision of Being. Habermas's concerns overlap with those of the pope only to a degree: for him, defending human nature means halting the reduction of human life, the body, embryos, the genetic code, and so on to commodities susceptible of being patented and bought and sold on the market. For the pope, it is a question of keeping faith with the essence of the human being that God the

creator established. But the Church used exactly the same rationale to hinder biologists from performing autopsies in the Middle
Ages, and there has never been a time when it didn't oppose the
efforts of scientists to know nature better and to manipulate it
with technology for the good of humanity. This is why the Church
is so heavily invested in sexuality; one of the latest public pronouncements from the conference of Italian bishops states that
sexuality as far as they are concerned is something "that cannot
be changed," a sort of natural limit that has to be observed even
if, or because, it cannot be changed. What we have here is the cus-
tomary naturalistic error on which so much of Catholic ethics is
based, a clear violation of what is known as Hume's Law, in that it
derives a norm from a fact. Now that it is becoming increasingly
possible to change even this aspect of nature, and the "natural
fact" is no longer a fact, where do we seek the will of God? All
these observations on sexuality, nature, and the will of God are
closely linked to nihilism and postmodernity. The point of view
that I have been advancing here is that nihilism is the postmodern interpretation, or version, of Christianity—in my opinion the
only one that can save it from ebbing away to nothing or ending
violently in a universal religious conflict. To put it another
way: the death of God proclaimed by Nietzsche is nothing more
than the death of Jesus on the cross. In Nietzsche, the death of
God signifies the final dissolution of supreme values and metaphysical belief in an objective and eternal order of Being. That is
nihilism in a nutshell. This is not the place to spell out how Heidegger develops the concept of nihilism in the context of his theory of the end of metaphysics. I would point out, though, that his
struggle against metaphysics was more than theoretical, since it

was ethically motivated by a refusal to accept the totalitarian social and political order (*die totale Verwaltung*, in Frankfurt parlance) that was coming about as metaphysics culminated in positivism and scientism.

Nihilism equals Christianity because Jesus came into the world not to demonstrate what the "natural" order was but to demolish it in the name of charity. Loving one's enemies is not exactly what nature prescribes, and more than that it isn't what "naturally" happens. So when the Church defends the natural order of the monogamous reproductive family against any act of charity whatsoever toward (naturally) gay persons or bars women from the priesthood (once again, because women are supposed to have a different natural vocation), it shows its preference for the God of the natural order over the message of Jesus. It is no surprise that a Church oriented in that way is also "naturally" reactionary, always defending the (dis)order in place except when it infringes on specific rights of the clergy: the history of Italy in the late nineteenth century and the Lateran Pacts between the Church and the Italian State in 1929, are textbook examples. Gioacchino da Fiore (Joachim of Fiore) was a true prophet when he taught in the Middle Ages that the history of salvation passes through moments and phases. Adapting his terminology, we could say that we are living in the age of the Spirit, which is as much as to say that we are living in an epoch that through science and technology can dispense with metaphysics and a metaphysical God: a nihilist epoch. An epoch in which our religiosity can finally develop into the form of charity no longer dependent on truth. There is no longer any reason to say, "Plato a friend but the truth a greater friend." In the past, the Church (the Churches, rather) put a whole range of heretics to death for just the reason encapsulated in that phrase. There is not, and ought not to be, anything more than charity, a welcoming, toward the other.

But back to our topic. In the age of the Spirit, the age of the end of metaphysics, why on earth should Christian believers still be worried about the "natural order"? With the mists of objective, authoritarian, reactionary metaphysics dissipated, the natural order is simply the way things usually go. Bear in mind that even a still metaphysical thinker like Kant based the need for a life after death on his rejection of the ethical disorder we see in nature.

But what about God the creator? One of the main points of contention between Christian thought and science (modern and indeed premodern) has always been the question of creation. Is it still? Are we still meant to believe that Jesus was persuaded that he was *the* son of God the creator of the world? Today there is a broad swathe of agreement that even the qualification of God as Father can be demythologized without causing the Christian faith to crumble. Why shouldn't the same hold good when it comes to the origin of the material world? There is truth to the positivist claim that the development of the natural sciences gradually causes the field of theology to shrink. Research into the origins of the material world is a scientific matter, like the laws of astronomy and the alternative between the Ptolemaic and Copernican models. The Bible is not a manual of natural science; even the Church now concedes that, having lifted the condemnation of Galileo. Just think how different the Christian faith could be if it weren't saddled with the mission of defending a specific description of the way the world came about.

The inevitable atheistic impact of modern cosmological knowledge about things like the time scale of the physical world, the possible multiplicity of universes, and extraterrestrial life would practically disappear. The Christian revelation is about just one thing, the possible salvation of our souls—not in terms of physical survival but rather as experience of the fullness of earthly life illuminated by a hope of resurrection, the Parousia. How many Christians today still believe literally in a life after death, pictured as a continuation of this one but enhanced with eternal beatitude or eternal punishment? "The kingdom of God is among you" (Luke 17:21) may perfectly well mean that eternal life in grace is something available to experience here and now. I am on record as combating the atheistic impact of modern cosmology by rejecting the claims to objectivity and hence truth of experimental natural science. It functions on the basis of paradigms that are wrongly taken as if they were "a gaze from nowhere." Science's linguistic game is completely detached from that of religion, and neither can arrogate to itself the right to the last word. I still hold that view, but I am prepared to concede that my stance vis-à-vis the objectivity of the natural sciences is free to be a lot less rigid once I have fully absorbed the fact that scientific cosmology poses no threat to my faith. In many ways, what the Catholic Church is doing today in relation to sexuality, and generally in its entrenched defense of "nature" (see above *passim* on the family, genetic engineering, biblical anthropology), is the same thing it did against Galileo and Copernican cosmology. The pope insists on imposing a vision of the natural world that is continually controverted by science, as in creationism versus Darwinism. It is entirely possible that Darwinism might be controverted, but certainly not on the basis of the literal truth of the text of the Old Testament.

Can we really do without biblical mythology, New Testament or Old? I don't believe so. I wouldn't want a Church without saints or Christmas and Easter rituals. But I don't want to be compelled to accept an elaborate doctrine like transubstantiation just so I can go to Mass. To take Christian mythology as though it were a description of a reality alternative to that of science is an authoritarian abuse that the Church ought to abandon, because it scandalizes the faithful.

Back to sexuality. Like the institution of the family in history, sexuality too has undergone profound transformations in terms of cultural practices and the freedom of individuals. Why, for example, should a Christian not accept that one is free to change one's sex? As for the kinds of abuse that cause Habermas enough concern to turn him "papist," let's try to be clear. Habermas thinks it would be a violation of nature, of the "natural" liberty of the infant, if he or she were genetically engineered to be predisposed to, or adept at, some activity like music or flying airplanes. But on that basis, we ought also to prevent parents from intervening in any direct way to keep an infant from being born with a disease or some grave deformity. Examples like that reveal that it is impossible and inhuman to decide bioethical questions on the basis of "respect for nature." Such criteria may be helpful, but it is increasingly evident that Habermas's worries can really only be met through concrete legislation based primarily on the consensus of all those directly concerned. I know that sounds too simplistic and limited, but a detailed inquiry into the matter would show that it is possible to establish proper norms in bioethics without reference to vague criteria like "nature."

Let us begin with a few remarks that may help us to understand what interpretation signifies and what its role is in the ensemble of what we call knowledge. In the act of knowing, I always select a perspective. What about scientists? They have chosen to set aside their private interests, but they describe only that which their scientific field encompasses, so they never know everything. On the other hand, a map that coincides exactly with the terrain it maps is entirely pointless.

Heidegger's objection to metaphysics also begins here, with the observation that even in deciding to be objective, we always assume a definite, *defined* position, a vantage point or viewpoint that delimits but that is also indispensable for our encounter with the world. Heidegger's critique of metaphysics as a claim to define the truth as an objective datum starts from that observation and then goes on to focus on the ethicopolitical aspects of metaphysics: the "rationalized" society of the early twentieth century against which the historical avant-gardes of the time struggled. Heidegger realized that even the pretended objectivity of the sciences is inspired by a determinate interest, such as to describe the movement of gases in such a way that others will be able to discuss it too and advance knowledge of the behavior of gases; Lukács says the same from a Marxist perspective. Scientists are not driven by an impulse of truth, and it is not possible to imagine the relation between the world and knowledge as the world and the mirror of the world. Rather, we imagine it as the world and someone who stands in the world and takes his bearings in it utilizing his cognoscitive capacities, in other words choosing, reorganizing, substituting, and so on.

The whole concept of interpretation lies right there. There is no experience of truth that is not interpretive; I know nothing unless it interests me, but if it interests me, evidently I don't gaze upon it in a disinterested fashion. In Heidegger, this concept enters into his thinking about the historical sciences, as one sees in the early sections of *Being and Time* and in many other texts from the same period. Hence I am an interpreter inasmuch as I do not gaze upon the world from outside; I gaze on the world outside me precisely because I am inside it. If I am inside it, however, my interest is far from straightforward. I cannot state exactly how matters stand, only how they look from where I stand, how they appear to me, and how I believe them to be. If I have an idea that leads to a successful experiment, that doesn't mean that I gained exhaustive, objective knowledge of that aspect of reality. What I did—and the philosophy of science backs this up—was to make the experiment work, on the basis of certain expectations and premises. When I do an experiment, I already dispose of a set of criteria and instruments that make it possible for me, and for anyone whose ideas differ from mine, to tell whether the experiment worked or not. The criteria and the instruments are already in place and undisputed when I start. No scientist studies all of physics from scratch; they all learn from textbooks and build on that. This is universally accepted. So I don't want to hear any more of this talk about how scientists describe the world objectively. They describe it with rigorous instruments, which are nonetheless determined and historically qualified. I would even hazard, knowing full well that this proposition will not command universal assent, that the possibility of verifying a scientific proposition, or falsifying it (as Popper would say, but in this case it comes to the same thing), depends on the fact that we use the same language, use analogous instruments, take the same measurements, etc. Otherwise we could not communicate at all. We didn't invent this ensemble of premises and paradigms from scratch; we inherited it. All this is interpretation: being within a situation and confronting it like someone who didn't arrive from Mars five minutes ago but who has a history, belongs to a community. Some maintain that to study physics is not to study the truth of physics; that it's more like being trained to become a member of a secret, or public, society. That's not so far fetched: to get someone to understand a scientific demonstration, you first have to teach her the rudiments. Are these rudiments natural knowledge, or are they knowledge of a particular science that could also be different? All this is mixed up with cultural anthropology and structuralism. Heidegger was not yet acquainted with the structuralism of Levi-Strauss, but what was going on in the interval between Kant and Heidegger? The whole nineteenth century, with the discovery that cultures vary widely, and the beginnings of the scientific study of them. Cultural anthropology goes back to the second half of the nineteenth century. According to Kant, to know the world humans require certain a priori, as he calls them, structures that we cannot derive from experience and through which we organize experience. To use a down-to-earth simile, I learn to see by discovering a pair of eyes, but I already need a set of eyes to discover them.

Space, time, and the linked categories of judgment are part of me; like my eyes, they are structures of reason. Overall, though, Kant and many neo-Kantian philosophers have always taken it for granted that reason was unvarying. Cultural anthropology brings about a more mature discourse about the differences among the structures with which cultures, societies, and different individuals confront the world. At bottom, Heidegger's twentieth-century existentialism may be viewed as Kantianism that has undergone cultural anthropology. As a finite being, I am born and die at certain points in history. How can I possibly be the bearer of the sort of absoluteness that would allow me to assert that two plus two indubitably make four? There are peoples who consume human flesh, and European thought exhibits an array of differences. Early cultural anthropology accepted the existence of other cultures but classified them as cultures "preceding" our own. In short, the primitives don't yet know mathematics, but we arrive in their countries, teach them science, and install our governments. Where are the "primitives" now? Who is there still willing to heed that narrative?

Let me put it this way: interpretation is the idea that knowledge is not the pure mirroring of the datum but an interested approach to the world using schemes that have varied over time. And that is supposed to extend even to Christianity? How did a philosopher ever go so far as to posit that? According to other philosophers with whom Heidegger was fairly closely linked, like Dilthey, the first blow of the hammer against the edifice of metaphysics as objectivity was delivered by Christianity. In his view, Kant realized centuries later what Christianity had asserted as early as Saint Augustine, that *in interiore homine habitat veritas*, that truth resides within the individual human being. It is pointless to strive to view the order of the ideas the way Plato did: the objectivity, the beauty of the cosmos, and so on. That won't save us; we save ourselves only by directing our gaze inward and seeking the profound truth within ourselves. With that, according to Dilthey (Heidegger never comes out and says so, but he always accepts this sketch of the history of philosophy), there commences an attention to subjectivity that entails things like the redemption of the poor. The modern world's literary realism is seen by Erich Auerbach (1946) as an expression of Christianity, which is a religion of intimacy, and so, tendentially, the intimacy of every man and woman. Hence each of us is equal to every other. For that matter, the philosophies of late antiquity are a bit like that: Epicureanism and Stoicism are more subject-oriented philosophies. It is certainly true that it is Christianity that in many ways undermines the peremptoriness of the object and favors attention to the subject. And so, says Dilthey, we arrive at Kant: truth lies not in things, which always present as random, but in human reason and its schemes, and in coming to perceive them we become aware that knowledge of truth is something we make. Today philosophers of science tell us that individual phenomena (the pot of water that boils at one hundred degrees centigrade) are not better known, as individual phenomena, when science manages to generalize them in formulas. In generating mathematical formulas, science transcends the individual phenomenon after a fashion and locates it within an entirely artificial system. In other words, a thermometer doesn't help me to know the boiling of water better; it helps me to generalize about the matter within a broader framework. Abstraction is not a way of peering deep into the phenomenon and perceiving its essence, as medieval science, with its Aristotelian roots, maintained (up to a point anyway). The essence at which we arrive is the general structure of a certain world of phenomena, which becomes true in some way when one steps back from individuality. I don't stand there watching the pot forever; I take measurements, correlate them, and create a system. This, once again, is fundamentally a Kantian mode of thought. With respect to the immediacy of that which I perceive,

I construct a system composed of linkages, connections, and calculations: all this is truth for Kant. In the wake of cultural anthropology and thought on the finiteness of existence, mathematics too may be just a mathematics. Early in the twentieth century there appeared alternative mathematics, non-Euclidean geometries. Why someone came up with these things I do not know, but they are evidently systems, logicomathematical constructs that work and in which it is possible to demonstrate theorems. When it turns out that they may account for certain natural phenomena more adequately than others (we are given to understand that certain non-Euclidean geometries are a better fit with cosmic space), we start to see that there may exist various languages that treat different phenomena differently.

Wittgenstein, whom you couldn't call an ally of Heidegger (I don't believe Heidegger ever read him), says for example that if someone presents me with a calculation that yields results different from mine, it is always licit to wonder whether he has miscalculated or whether he wasn't using a different mathematical language. This is already halfway to an acceptance of the idea of interpretation. So it isn't true that if we accept the prevalence of interpretation, anything goes and anyone can say whatever they please. The rules don't vanish, but they are the rules that apply in that language: in a nutshell, it's the whole discourse of the later Wittgenstein about linguistic games, in which every language is like a game with its own rules. If science were poker, you couldn't play it by the rules of bridge, and if you tried it would be possible to establish that you were making a mistake and violating the norms. But that doesn't mean that poker is the only game there is. Many historians of philosophy assert that this has been made possible in the modern world by the advent of Christianity.

I might also attempt to argue the point in a less philosophically refined way, like this: Thomas Aquinas knew perfectly well that Aristotle believed in the eternity of the world, and he acknowledged that that would be the more rational belief to hold. But from the point of view of biblical revelation, it was impossible: if you are going to preach a religion of free creation, salvation, grace, and miracles, then objectivity goes out the window, because definitive, metaphysical objectivity is the structure that, once discovered, we know (and cannot not know) to be the way it is (and cannot not be). So Christianity is a doctrine of interpretation for numerous reasons. One of them is that it trains its gaze inward and, so the historians of ideas tell us, brings it about that we gradually come to understand subjectivity in a Kantian manner. Basically, if it is possible to theorize this today, it is so because we live in a Christian civilization, albeit no longer in Christianity in the full sense. The whole creation myth in the Bible runs right up against the compact metaphysics of Plato, Aristotle, and the rest. And it is not alone. In the New Testament there is that extravagant episode of the descent of the Holy Spirit upon the Virgin Mary and the apostles . . . what's that about? It answers Christ's promise in the Johannine gospel: "I have said these things to you while still with you; but the Advocate, the Holy Spirit, whom the Father will send in my name, will teach you everything and remind you of all I have said to you" (14:25–26). This, as I see it, justifies the historical transformation of Christian truth: the message of Christianity is true because Christ presents himself as one who is there to interpret a preceding scripture (what we call the Old Testament), and the Old Testament itself is highly mysterious. It is hard to believe that Moses was inscribing his tables while God was dictating them to him from on high. No one would assert that hermeneutics starts with the New Testament, because the entire Old Testament, and Hebraism in general, are the fruit of the interpretation and reinterpretation of the writings. Walter Benjamin, for example, one of the great figures of twentieth-century philosophy, thought everything in Talmudic terms, meaning in terms of commentary on some message that had been handed down. So the origins of the idea of interpretation always lie somewhere farther back in the past. Even the evangelists did not write their accounts before 60 C.E., a good few years after the death of Jesus. One of the reasons Heidegger decided to comment on the Letter to the Thessalonians in his course on the phenomenology of religion in 1920–1921 was because it is the oldest known New Testament writing, predating the gospels by a long shot. This doesn't mean a great deal, except that the gospels too (which we take as unalterable scripture) are already written accounts of teachings previously transmitted orally in the Christian community.

What do I take from this jumble of considerations (which reflect my reading of René Girard as well as Heidegger)? That Christianity is a stimulus, a message of liberation from metaphysics. It is something eternal. So metaphysics should never have existed and Aristotle was one hundred percent wrong? I withhold judgment about that, because any reasoning about the matter would be typically metaphysical. It would lead to maintaining that it is eternally true that metaphysics is an error. That I cannot say, nor can I say virtually anything else except by responding to messages of words, of tradition. Someone might ask, "but why are you so convinced that you should be preaching this to us if you are not a metaphysician?" To which I would reply, "but haven't you read a, b, c, and d?" In short, the only arguments I can adduce are not ones of the traditional type but ones of transmission, language, the classics we have in common. When I say that I am convinced that God created me, I am able only to think that without the text (and the textual history) of the Bible, my life as a thinking being at this moment would have no sense. It would be like removing Dante from the history of Italian literature, but Dante's works are composed in such a way that if you haven't read the Bible, you don't understand a thing, whereas the Bible you can read without having read either Dante or Shakespeare. The point is that to profess faith in Christianity is first and foremost to profess faith in the ineluctability of a certain textuality that has been passed down to us. I wouldn't be what I am; perhaps I'd be something else, but it's no use trying to imagine what it would be like to be, let's say, a native of Amazonia. If I reflect on my existence, I am forced to acknowledge that without biblical textuality, I wouldn't possess instruments for thinking and speaking. There's a phrase in Benedetto Croce that I often comment on, bending it this way and that: "we cannot not call ourselves Christians." We cannot speak ourselves otherwise than as Christians, because we are unable to formulate ourselves, meaning we are unable to articulate a discourse within our culture without accepting certain premises.

What about Voltaire? Voltaire was a good Christian: he defended liberty against authoritarianism, including that of the eighteenth-century Jesuits. That's why Christianity must be non-religious, perhaps. Christianity has latent powers to liberate, and that, I make bold to say, includes liberation from the truth. If there is an objective truth, there will always be someone nearer to it than I am, someone who will arrogate to themselves the right and the duty to impose it on me. Everywhere you look, you see authoritarianism grounded in claims of a metaphysical kind, and authoritarian government displays little inclination to make the case for its policies on the basis of rational self-interest. If one had been able to say to Bush that the war in Iraq was a high-risk venture, his baffled reply would have been: "But Saddam is a bad guy." That Saddam was a bad guy is a point one may concede, but the criteria of who's bad and good are Bush's. Even UN resolution 1441 is just a UN Security Council resolution: it was passed by the victors of the Second World War, not the Heavenly Father. It may be the only form of global legality we have, but that doesn't make it sacrosanct. Therefore, on the basis of this code, we can wage preventive war.

If Christianity did not set us free from objective truth, would you really be able to believe, even in part, even allegorically, what the Holy Scripture says? These days I often cite a Turinese colleague of mine as a bad example: he wrote a book in which he calculated the height that the Virgin Mary must have reached by now in her vertical bodily ascent into heaven. She was taken up in bodily form, but what was her velocity and point of arrival? Why didn't she just vanish in a flash? To believe in the gospels, you have to believe that language does more than just denote objective reality. There is another language too, which says different things, which speaks precisely about those famous paradigms on the basis of which we interpret nature objectively. It's like when I say that to know, to prove, a scientific proposition I require preliminary instruments. But I don't make those instruments in turn the object of scientific scrutiny, because to do that I would need yet another set of instruments preliminary to the preliminary ones, and so on in an infinite regress. Likewise I use the language that I have inherited to speak about values, about projects, about coherence. I cannot speak outside of a certain linguistic tradition, a certain encyclopedia, a certain dictionary, and these are the bases of my existence. Thus I can understand the language of the gospels too as that which communicates to me something that is not ontic, is not given in the physical world, doesn't even demand a realistic interpretation, but speaks (to me) of my destiny. When someone says "I love you," the words "I love you" don't describe any objective phenomenon. That person might answer that it does, "because I can feel my pulse pounding when I think of my beloved." But is that really supposed to be the objectivity of the phrase "I love you"?

What is the case, is that this discourse about interpretation, about existence, matures in a historical progression that is also the historical progression of Western culture and science. Until Galileo it wasn't so easy to be Kantian in science, in the sense that Aristotelian scientists, to caricature matters a bit, collected all the turtles and then built the theory of the turtle, without quantification. Only with modern science, with Bacon and Galileo above all, is this world constructed in a way that seems made to order for the philosophy of Kant and also tailored to confirm something that Dilthey says about Christianity achieving awareness of human action on the world. Where are we headed? We are headed for secularization, another name for which is nihilism, the idea that objective Being has gradually consumed itself. Nietzsche's beautiful page from *Twilight of the Idols* about "How the Real World at Last Became a Myth" tells a story, starting with the idea of the real world, the world of the Platonic ideas. Then the real world becomes the world promised to the righteous after death (paradise), and then it becomes the world of Descartes, with the evidentness of clear and distinct ideas (but only in my mind; if God is there to protect me from error, they are also true). The succeeding stage is positivism, the world of truths experimentally verified, hence produced in an experiment by the experimenters. And I do mean produced: it is ever more difficult to imagine the scientific experimenter as one who contemplates nature; he twists it and pokes it and prods it, with the aim of achieving certain things. At this point, the world has become a story told among ourselves. All this may be hard to accept, but we are living in a world of that kind. We no longer see nature; we see mainly our world, organized by an ensemble of entities of a technological sort. When we refer to our "natural" needs, we include things like elevators and the cinema, which have indeed become natural needs for us, though they aren't. If it's a choice between that and survival in a world where it's just you ranging through the forest with an animal skin around your loins, you are unlikely to opt to switch. Our natural needs are all those in which we are immersed, most of which are not in the least natural but are conditioned by advertising, stimulated by technology, and so on. We are living in a world that has become mythical and fabulous in countless ways. If you see a traffic accident, you run home and turn on the television to find out what happened, because you couldn't see clearly what was going on from where you were standing on the sidewalk. And this is what we are living every day. That the real world has become a fable can also be expressed in terms of Nietzsche's nihilism. The objectivity of our world has (luckily) self-consumed, giving way to an ever-widening subjective transformation, not so much at the level of the individual as at that of communities, cultures, sciences, languages. This is what I try to theorize with weak thought. If there is a possible thread of emancipation in human history, it doesn't lie in finally realizing an essence given at the outset for all time. Are we supposed to try to be like the idea of mankind before original sin? Christianity is full of conflicting interpretations about that. What we must do is simply realize an ever greater transformation of the natural into the cultural, or the material into the spiritual. This is what Hegel meant when he spoke of making the world into a dwelling for mankind. You don't just strew the furniture about in your home; you put things where they belong, and when something is missing you know it immediately. It is an artificial order founded by you. Baudelaire wrote, "wherever I have seen virtue, I have seen counter-nature." That gets it exactly. Nature is the world where the big fish eat the little fish, not in the least a place where natural laws and rights obtain. Virtue is the complete opposite: it is culture, meaning something that transcends nature. Emancipation basically lies in taking secularization further, in the sense of grasping better and better the spiritual sense of Scripture. We have learned to read the Holy Scriptures spiritually. Max Weber proposed that the capitalist world was generated primarily by a certain version of the Protestant ethic: reinvestment and repression of the impulse to consume immediately were fundamental for capital accumulation. The modern world was formed by applying and transforming, and sometimes also mistaking, the content of our tradition, principally the biblical tradition. How far are we authorized to take this transformation? Are we free to do whatever we please? No, because in Scripture we also find a limit to secularization in the discourse of charity, the very thing that guides desacralization. If you read the gospels and the Church fathers, in the end the sole virtue that remains is always charity. Even faith and hope end sooner or later. Saint Augustine said, "love and do what you want," which isn't all that undemanding a precept, since if you follow it strictly, everything that isn't charity is just mythology. I do not know if God is really one person and three persons at the same time. We are told that it is indispensable to believe that he is, but we no longer burn those who don't for trinitarian heresy. We may try to convince them otherwise if we like. For that matter, no one guarantees us that God is a father or a mother or a family member of any other kind; it is clearly allegorical language. Once this point of view becomes pervasive, you feel consternation, because you don't know where it stops. For example, can someone like me still recite the Lord's Prayer? Yes, because when I pray I know perfectly well that I am using words that I cannot use literally, words I use more out of love for the tradition in which I stand than out of love for reality. It would be like expecting an eighty-year-old aunt to share my political ideas on interpersonal relationships. I don't bother her about things like that, and indeed when I am speaking in her presence I respect old-fashioned decency in language, a respect inspired by charity, in disregard of any imperative to speak the truth. It isn't even transparently clear why scientists remain inside the scientific community: is it because they love the truth or because their insider status allows them to develop their thinking and supplies them with interlocutors? Today we have a philosopher like Habermas affirming that rationality consists of presenting arguments that may decently be defended before others; he doesn't say that what's rational or possibly true is what comes from deep inside me or what corresponds to "the thing in itself." Saint Augustine only got halfway to an adequate definition of truth as I see it. Granted, his precept "look within yourself" is an advance on the truth of the object. But if you turn toward your inner self, oughtn't you also try to heed "the other as yourself"?

Today, on many topics, we are unable to state the truth except when we reach agreement with others. Here's a formula that sums up the notion: we don't reach agreement when we have discovered the truth, we say we have discovered the truth when we reach agreement. In other words, charity takes the place of truth. Dostoevsky writes: "If I had to choose between Jesus Christ and truth, I would choose Jesus Christ."

It is in this sense that when the word "truth" is uttered, a shadow of violence is cast as well. Not all metaphysicians have been violent, but I would say that almost all large-scale perpetrators of violence have been metaphysicians. If Hitler had merely hated the Jews in his neighborhood, he would have set fire to their houses, and that would have been it. But he worked up a general theory to the effect that they were an inferior race and that it would be better to eliminate them completely. In other words, he reached the point of holding a theory that he believed to be true. This is not hard to understand. Nietzsche doesn't mince words; he says that metaphysics is an act of violence that wants to appropriate "the most fertile regions" for itself, meaning the first principles that allow it to dominate all the consequences. The first lines of Aristotle's *Metaphysics* say more or less the same thing: the wise man is the all-knowing man, and he knows all because he knows the primary causes, which allows him to control the effects. Our tradition is overshadowed by the idea that if we can get a grip on a stable entity, then we can finally act at will. We fix a stable entity because we want to obtain some effect or demonstrate it authoritatively and lastingly to others. Anyone claiming to tell me the absolute truth is demanding from me unquestioning submission. Where does this discourse lead with respect to Christianity?

Gadamer, it is often said, developed a religious attitude in his late years, a species of ecumenism. He focused a lot on interreligious dialogue and seemed to want to play a soothing role. That was fundamentally a good outcome for his hermeneutic discourse: if there is no truth objectively given once and for all to anyone around which everyone is supposed to form ranks willingly or not, then truth sprouts and blossoms in dialogue, because what Christ came to teach the Church was not yet all accomplished; it was there as a virtuality in his message, but the message expands with its applications in history. No one can read Plato in isolation from all the interpretations. It would be absurd, because you would fatally select the one that seemed most natural, but it would be historical like all the others. Italian teenagers who write poetry almost always sound like Pascoli. Nietzsche says that if there is something that looks absolutely self-evident to you, be on your guard, because it is undoubtedly some tale that has wormed its way into your head. The last thing you can be certain of is your most deeply rooted certainties, because those are the ones you were taught by your aunts and grandmothers, the Church, the authorities, the newspapers, advertising. Christianity is marching in a direction that can only be that of lightening and weakening its burden of dogma in favor of its practical and moral teaching. In that sense too, charity takes the place of truth. Are we really supposed to quarrel first with the Protestants and then eventually with the Buddhists and the Hindus, because they do not believe that God is three and one at the same time? When the pope meets the Dalai Lama, is he thinking that the Dalai Lama is going to hell because he isn't Catholic? No, they discuss things like how to raise the level of spirituality in humanity, and they probably agree on a good many things. The future of Christianity, and of the Church, is to become an ever more refined religion of pure charity. There is a hymn sung in church that goes: "Where charity and love are, there God is." Is that thought so extravagant? "When two or more of you are united in my name, I am with them"—and "in my name" may just be another way of saying, "in charity." That is the presence of God. So it is difficult to imagine that in the end we will be damned because some are Buddhists, others Muslims, and so on. We are damned, or damn ourselves, already here on earth when we fight murderously with one another, each believing that the true God is with him. This isn't just the usual message of tolerance: it's the ideal of the development of human society through the gradual reduction of all the rigidities that set us against one another, including the instinct of property, blood, family, and all the problems associated with the excessive absolutization, in defiance of charity, of things naturally given. The truth that sets us free is true precisely because it sets us free: if it doesn't free us, it is disposable. That is why I refuse to admit that weak thought, with all that it entails, is just a species of preaching of tolerance. It's the idea of a project for the future as the progressive elimination of walls—the Berlin Wall, the wall of natural laws that they preach against the freedom of individuals, the wall of the laws of the market . . . I believe that ecumenism is inconceivable except as a lightening of the burden of dogma and the wider preaching of charity. This is the discourse of hermeneutics, Gadamer's discourse, the discourse of much of the most reasonably acceptable contemporary philosophy.

FAITH IN EUROPE

The question of religious faith in Europe assumes particular urgency in connection with the creation of the European Union. On one hand, the common cultural, spiritual, and therefore religious roots of the peoples of the continent are advanced as an argument in favor of progressing toward an authentic federal European state. On the other, those who for various reasons prefer a slower process of unification or indeed a halt to any further progress toward integration often emphasize how in reality the various countries belonging geographically to Europe have differing cultures, which cannot be adduced as a factor promoting integration. And for that matter, in the recent flare-up of ethnic conflict, the former Yugoslavia being a case in point, religion, along with language and culture in general, played a strongly divisive role rather than a conciliatory one.

Now it is incontestable that Europe is not a nation in the nineteenth-century and Romantic sense of the term; it lacks a common language, and the historical roots of the tongues spoken on the continent are separated into Romance, Germanic, Slavic, and Finno-Ugric branches, to name only the main ones. Europe's Christian unity is just a medieval memory that was buried with the Protestant Reformation, if not before that, with the schism between the Catholic and Orthodox Churches. The ideal reasons that underlie the creation of a European federation therefore appear hard to reconcile with schematic nineteenth-century nationalism; indeed, the European Union is about consigning that idea of nationhood to the past once and for all. It may have inspired the struggle for independence and the birth of many European states that have become democracies, but it also produced detrimental and negative consequences. The union of Europe is inspired less by the idea of a profound spiritual unity that is putatively expressed even at the State level than by what I would call a negative ideal: that of putting in place bonds that will prevent the repetition of the wars that, in the past, saw the national states of Europe at one another's throats. European unity is, from that perspective, an entirely artificial idea, which cannot claim any natural basis, like the unity of a nation, a people, or a language. Europe isn't even clearly defined in geography; the expression "from the Atlantic to the Urals" is little more than a rhetorical flourish, which is already being nullified by the foreseeable membership of Turkey in the European Union. That's without even mentioning the countries on the southern shore of the Mediterranean Sea, which isn't and never has been a barrier between them and Europe at all, more of a broad highway of communication and integration.

The topic is complex, and it would take us far afield. But it should be borne in mind if we intend to inquire into what religion, which de facto means Christianity, signifies in the Europe of today and tomorrow. My point is that we cannot start with the premise that Christianity is one of the cultural factors of European unity, not at any rate in the sense that it defines a deep-rooted identity that would legitimize political unification, the way it did in the formation of the modern national states. The common and ramified Christian roots of Europe are at odds with the "artificial" character of the notion of European unity. It is true, in a very peculiar sense which I will try to illustrate, that European unity will inevitably be Christian. But only on condition of understanding Christianity not as a positive factor of identity but on the exact contrary, as a potent summons to disidentification. To put it a little differently, I would say that Christianity can contribute to the construction of a united Europe (and therefore a more pacific, democratic, and economically competitive Europe) only if it develops its own postmodern nature. I would also say, vice versa, that the political decision to construct a federal Europe obliges Christianity to acknowledge this postmodern vocation as its own. The historically consolidated profile of Christianity in Europe is that of a plurality of Churches, each strongly characterized in terms of dogma, discipline, and social rootedness, and in that guise it was for a long time, and still is, a force for division rather than a force for cohesion and unity. Are the wars of religion that tore Europe apart in the sixteenth and seventeenth centuries really locked away safely in the past? We tend to think so, but if it is true, to the extent that it is true, we owe it to the process of secularization that was given such a powerful impetus by the Enlightenment. But the fact is that in one way or another the Christian Churches, especially the Catholic Church (still the recognizable face of Christianity as far as most of the world is concerned), have never really accepted the process of secularization as a positive and liberating event. In other words, they haven't acknowledged what to many thinkers and theologians appears to be the well-established fact that the secularization of modern society is an effect of Christianity rather than a symptom of its waning and dissolution. Not much more than one hundred years ago the papacy, in the person of Pius IX, condemned liberalism and democracy as false and pernicious in his Syllabus of Errors. And speaking of errors, many political ones committed by the Roman Catholic Church in the twentieth century, starting with its attitude to fascism and Nazism, were motivated not just by contingent reasons of convenience but by deep mistrust of any form of "modernization," which it saw as a dangerous drift away from the sacred.

Certainly neither the Catholic Church, nor as far as I know any other Christian Church, has taken a stand against European unity. But the conviction that the unity of Europe can and should be founded on common acceptance of the Christian tradition is all too evident in the attitudes adopted by representatives of the ecclesiastical hierarchy and politicians promoting a Christian vision of the human species. There was a concrete example of this recently when the European Charter of Rights was being formulated, an event which, by the way, ought to have been celebrated with greater solemnity and awarded greater recognition than it was in the parliaments of the EU member states. Voices were raised in many quarters complaining that the preamble mentioned the "spiritual" heritage of the peoples of the European continent rather than the specifically religious, let alone Christian, heritage. The only explanation for this discontent is the claim that the basis of united Europe is the Christian tradition, in the sense of a set of positive dogmas—precisely the thing that shattered the unity of medieval Europe, precisely the thing that gave us the wars of religion, which had to be ended through imposed secularization. Christianity as a core of dogma cannot constitute the cultural basis of Europe's *modern* identity. We see this clearly enough in various European countries, not least Italy, where a large section of the ecclesiastical hierarchy is starting to speak about Christian identity as a patrimony that needs defending against the growth of the Islamic community, to which most immigrants in most European countries belong. The bishop (and cardinal) of a large Italian diocese recently asserted that in order for foreign immigrants who are Muslim to live at peace with Italians, they ought to be taught not just the rudiments of our language and culture but the Catholic religion as well. You could see it as a reprise of sorts of the Westphalian principle *cuius regio eius religio* (every sovereign state imposes religious uniformity within its borders), except that the bishop in question doesn't remotely imagine a situation of reciprocity, in which for instance Christians who emigrated to Saudi Arabia would have to become Muslim. The soil from which this idea springs, though for now it has only been floated as a vague but nonetheless significant and worrying hint, is the same missionary and colonial spirit that drove European imperialism for centuries.

I don't bring up these facts in a spirit of theological, let alone political, altercation. For me it is a matter of acknowledging that the only way for Christianity still to discharge its own historical vocation of constituting the foundational values of modern Europe is for it to think of itself and become (even at the cost of a profound transformation of the Church or Churches) a religion of the dissolution of the "sacred" and the expanding recognition of the sole principles of liberty and charity. The Vatican has taken some quite significant strides in this direction recently. The pope has requested pardon for the condemnation of Galileo, for all those burned at the stake by the Inquisition, for the persecutory attitude toward the "perfidious Jews" (as they were called until a few years ago in the Catholic liturgy), and even for the excommunication of Luther. But if the withdrawal of the condemnation of Copernican heliocentrism implies recognition of the fact that the Bible is not a manual of astronomy, why not go further and recognize that it is not a treatise in anthropology, morality, or even theology either? The New Testament speaks of God as father, and we still recite the Lord's Prayer with emotion. But are we really supposed to consider anathema the feminist objections to this masculinization of the divinity? When I posit that the Bible cannot be considered a theological treatise, meaning an ensemble of propositions on God, his existence, and his nature,[3] I am referring to that as well. It was over questions like the sex of the angels or whether or not the nature of God entails certain relations and not others among the persons of the Trinity that the Christian Churches split apart and went on to violate in the bloodiest way the fundamental (and the only immutable) evangelical precept of charity.

Readers will have observed that when I speak of Christianity as the dissolution of the sacred, one of my references is the theories of a great Christian thinker (who is certainly not in agreement with the implications I draw from his thought), René Girard. His thesis that the incarnation of Christ was nonsacrificial in character is decisive for the vision I am proposing here of Christianity as the religion of modern and postmodern Europe. God becomes man not as the adequate victim in reparation for sin but in order to reveal that the victim mechanism, the sacrifice, that characterizes the natural religions is something primitive, barbaric, a pure invention generated by the constitution of ordered societies, which need to release violence onto a victim, the scapegoat, because otherwise it would make life in society impossible. The Judeo-Christian revelation lies in the announcement that God is not violence but love, which is a scandalous announcement, so much so that Jesus was put to death for it. It is also an announcement so far exceeding the capacity of human knowledge that it could only have come from an incarnate God. If you read the Judeo-Christian revelation in these terms, which may be far from orthodox but are reasonable and well-grounded, you start to see that modern Europe, the processes of secularization, individual rights, freedom of conscience, political democracy—all of which were brought about against the explicit resistance of the Catholic Church and often the other Churches as well—are offshoots of the penetration of society by the Christian message. But not by the dogmas and the metaphysical conceptions that, it was claimed, had to be understood as necessarily bound to faith in Jesus Christ. Appearances to the contrary, Voltaire may have been a more authentic Christian than the Jesuits of his time. The Christianity that founded modern Europe is that of respect for the person, not that of smoldering pyres of heretics and witches. It was the religion of *caritas*, not that of the metaphysical, theological, and moral *veritates* which, it was thought, required acknowledgment on pain of heresy, excommunication, and damnation.

After all I have said, the meaning of the proposition I stated at the outset will be clearer, I hope. Christianity will be able to further the constitution of a united Europe, and ultimately perhaps a united world, only if it develops its own essence as a religion of charity and not of dogma, adopting a stance of openness to all religious cultures and mythologies, keeping faith with the spirit of hospitality and dissolution of the violence of the sacred that is the core of the preaching of Jesus. Nor is the creation of Europe the only source of pressure for such a transformation. But precisely the increasing political integration of our continent and in general the countless phenomena of globalization that are irresistibly coming about in our world are a providential event of sorts, summoning the Christian churches to consume (wear out, use up, finish off) their dogmatic claims and the whole train of metaphysical convictions about the nature of the world, God, and mankind they entail. By now all that is just fodder for religious authorities attempting to influence the legislative programs of governments. You can read this as the meaning of the title of the essay by Novalis, *Christianity or Europe* (1799). There is a linkage of destiny, a providential link, between the unfolding of European history, including the recent drive toward the political unification of the continent, and the fulfillment of the history of salvation announced in the Bible. It is this that, as Christians and Europeans, we need to have the courage to think through in the radical manner required.

THOUGHTS ON ETHICS

Anyone with questions about ethics on their mind, all those in quest of ethics, share a common hope: the expectation that ethics will yield binding principles.[1] The question spontaneously takes the form: "What (ought we) to do?" The word "duty" turns up more often than any other in discussions of ethics, and most people think it would be a meaningless word if it did not depend on some principle from which the answer "follows," like a logical consequence from logical premises. So failure to comply would be tantamount to rebelling against reason—against practical reason, that is, but the distinction between practical and theoretical reason is blurry at best, and from the intellectualistic point of view that seems to dominate most ethical philosophizing, it is probably hard to conceive why anyone would balk at acting rationally, in conformity with principles. The explanations advanced for such "irrational" behavior boil down to those foes of rationality, the passions and interests of human beings: all that the scholastics termed the "concupiscible" and associated with the least noble part of the human being, the body. The flesh will rot after death, but the soul belongs to the timeless realm of reason, because it has an essence like that of the eternal ideas.

Today, such premises to a discussion of ethics are seldom to be found in the philosophical literature, because reasoning on the basis of principles—meaning ultimate foundations, established, recognized, and intuited, from which one deduces logical and practical implications—has run its course. This is a matter of evident fact, not "principle." The crisis in ethics, which we hear described as one of the components, or the main component, of the debased standard of morality in public and private behavior, is the discredit into which "principled" reasoning in relation to grounds of universal validity has fallen. It is not hard to see that the universality and ultimacy of principles are one and the same. An ultimate ground or foundation is one lacking any ulterior conditions that in turn ground it. If it has no conditions, it is unconditional and can only present itself as an absolute truth that no one ought to be able to refuse (otherwise than through an ungrounded, irrational, pure act). When, as occurs in nineteenth- and twentieth-century thought, first principles come to be seen as secondary, preconditioned by something else like the ideological mechanisms of false consciousness, or the will to power, or the play of repression in the unconscious, the claim to universality collapses into discredit too. This discredit, which is not, I repeat, a probative refutation of some principle but rather an overall shift in the trend line, contingent and therefore riddled with exceptions, can only be characterized to a first approximation, not definitively backed up with irrefutable arguments. It is connected to the spread of cultural pluralism, which, partly as a consequence of the altered political relationship between the West and other cultural areas that have gone from the status of colonies to that of independent nations, has cast into relief the partiality of what for centuries European philosophy regarded as the essence of *humanitas*; it is also connected to the critique of ideology originated by Marxism, to the discovery of the unconscious by Freud, and to the radical demythification to which Nietzsche subjected traditional morality and metaphysics, up to and including the ideal of truth itself. Moreover, none of these "schools of suspicion" was itself the fruit of pure speculative contemplation; they all accompanied, if not simply mirrored, profound social transformations. Any reasonableness and theoretical validity they may have cannot even be argued for except by alluding to these historical circumstances and showing that a philosophy that dispenses with first principles, that indeed comes about precisely as a theoretical reckoning with the ungroundedness of thought, is the most appropriate (most verisimilar, most harmonious) response to the epoch of late modern pluralism.

To co-respond to the epoch is also a form of responsible commitment, so the lost aura of dutifulness does remain behind as a trace or imprint, allowing us to speak of a rationality and an ethics, meaning a commitment to derive logical consequences and practical imperatives from certain principles (here merely in the sense of points of departure). Were a reader to remark that this just repeats the schema of metaphysical ethics, in which you recognize the principles, articulate them rationally, and deduce from them the implications for action, she would be perfectly correct—with the proviso that here the metaphysical mechanism is reprised and twisted awry, following a logic that Heidegger descried and theorized under the name *Verwindung*, which repeats metaphysical logic while radically altering its meaning.

Metaphysical ethics, for example, fatally falls victim to the critique, known as Hume's Law, that it is illicit to move, as metaphysics does, with no explicit justification, from the description of how matters in fact stand to the formulation of a moral principle. When someone tells me to "be a man," he isn't commanding me to be that which I naturally am; he is really commending certain virtues that as far as he is concerned, must (but why?) define essential maleness. Examples of a similar kind abound. Well then: an ethics "responsible" to its own epoch and ungrounded in first principles is immune, or virtually immune, to Hume's Law, because the "how matters in fact stand" to which it is trying to correspond doesn't exist objectively; it is the whole manifold of our cultural inheritance, and it is only representable through a responsible act of interpretation, which does not yield incontrovertible imperatives.

If philosophy can still speak rationally of ethics, meaning in a way responsible to the sole referents that matter—the epoch, our historical inheritance, provenance—it can do so only by assuming as its explicit point of departure (not its foundation or ground) the condition of ungroundedness in which it now finds itself thrown. The overriding traits of provenance and inheritance (but what else do they override, and why?) amount precisely to the dissolution of first principles, the onset of an nonunifiable plurality. Is it possible to develop an ethical discourse (principles from which follow maxims of action, guidelines for conduct, rankings of values) on the basis of a provenance or epochal situatedness characterized as the dissolution of foundations? This dissolution may be more than just a matter of fact, the setting in which we happen to find ourselves thinking, or rather, being the setting in which foundational grounds came to an end, it becomes itself the only "ground," very *sui generis* to be sure, very much *verwunden*, available to us if we are to debate ethics at all. Metaphysics didn't leave us utterly orphaned: its dissolution (which

Nietzsche dramatizes in the little tale about the death of God) turns out to be a process endowed with a logic of its own, from which elements for a reconstruction may be extracted. I am talking about what Nietzsche called nihilism, which is not just the nihilism of the dissolution of all principles and values but also an active nihilism, the chance to begin a different history.

But what is there to be extracted, in terms of ethics (maxims of action, guidelines for behavior, rankings of values), from the recognition (interpretive, already fraught with responsible choices) of our belonging to a tradition characterized as the dissolution of principles? The first trait of an ethics of this sort can be thought of as a stepping back, a distancing of ourselves from the concrete choices and options that, in the near term and at short range, the situation seems to dictate. Admittedly, if there are no first, supreme, universal principles, the only imperatives that would seem to count are those imposed by specific situations, but right here is where the difference looms between a postmetaphysical ethics and relativism pure and simple (assuming that there could ever be such a thing): the constatation that the credibility of first principles has evaporated does not translate into the assumption of our historical condition and of our belonging to a community as the only absolute. If the real world (the first principles) has become a fable, writes Nietzsche, then the fable too has been destroyed (and so cannot be absolutized in turn).

The situation to which we really, first and foremost, belong and toward which we are responsible in our ethical choices is that characterized by the dissolution of principles, by nihilism. To take more specific attachments, to things like race, ethnicity, family, or social class, as one's ultimate references means limiting one's perspective right from the outset. Such a limitation is really just a repetition of the metaphysical game of first principles, in which a specific and particular fable is taken for the real world, in an act of ideological absolutization. Yet against such an iteration of metaphysics there is no absolute imperative that I could invoke. All I can do is propose a broadening of horizons, something along the lines of: if you agree that the reference for ethics is provenance, I invite you not to avert your gaze from the manifold of things that this provenance comprises.

But neither is it a case of taking everything into account, as though it might ever be possible to construct a complete inventory of what goes to make up the provenance toward which we are responsible. Characterizing our provenance as the dissolution of principles, as nihilism, can never lead to the definition of a new, more valid, principle. What we have at our disposal here is just the basis for a critical stance vis-à-vis all that claims to present itself as an ultimate and universal principle. Note that not even this stance can think of itself as universally valid, as a precept applicable to everyone always. It recognizes itself as appropriate to a certain condition—the one that Heidegger calls the epoch in which metaphysics ends but won't go away, the one that Nietzsche calls the epoch in which the news of God's demise hasn't yet reached the ears of a great many people and its consequences will require centuries to unfold.

The modern philosophical tradition supplies significant elements of support for this thesis, above and beyond Hume's Law. Foremost among them is Kantian ethical formalism, with its imperative to adopt only maxims of action that may hold good as universal norms (doing what we would want anyone else to do in the same situation). Here, of course, universality is not attributed positively to certain set contents but functions only as an admonition not to assume any specific contents that may appear cogent under particular circumstances (inclinations, interests, etc.) as ultimate principles.

Of course, we come back to the initial question or quest: what can be extracted, in terms of maxims of action and rankings of values, from the assumption of responsibility in the face of the dissolution of principles?

The risk of stepping back, of taking our distance from concrete alternatives, is that it may give rise to a relativistic metaphysics—a stance that can perfectly well be labeled metaphysical, inasmuch as only from a position solidly located in some universal point of view can (or could) one gaze on multiplicity as multiplicity. Relativism amounts to the metaphysical rigidification, self-contradictory and impracticable, of finiteness. Only God could be an authentic relativist. If the step back with respect to the alternatives given in the situation is meaningful, that isn't because it is possible or obligatory to locate oneself in a superior and universal perspective but because it is the situation itself, viewed without hasty metaphysical closure (interpreted with an effort to take into account its composite and open character), that demands a distancing from the spuriously ultimate alternatives it presents.

Only by working through this complicated knot of concepts, I believe, can a responsible philosophy address ethics today. Am I insisting on a stance too remote and abstract from everyday experience? I will answer that with another question: isn't the sensation of being extraneous to the concrete alternatives into which we find ourselves thrown already a constitutive trait of our everyday experience? Why should we resign ourselves to viewing this sensation as a purely individual psychological fact and not as a "civilizational unease" that deserves better than just being brushed away?

What is at stake, however one proceeds down this path of reasoning, is the assumption of the dissolution of principles as the point of departure toward a nonmetaphysical ethics advancing no claim, even surreptitiously, to construct itself as the practical application of a theoretical certainty concerning ultimate foundations. Even the sort of relativism that would make the step backward into a straightforward suspension of assent, a justification of blasé intellectual disengagement (there are numerous examples in today's philosophy, often of phenomenological origin and sounding much like the *epoché* theorized by Husserl), is just another way of tumbling back into the metaphysics of principles. Why? For the reason I have stated: it pretends to locate itself in a universal and completely stable point of view.

If, however, one does wish to co-respond to the dissolution of principles, there appears to be no other way than that of an ethics explicitly constructed around finiteness, understood neither as the compulsion to leap into the void (much twentieth-century religious thought argues this line: acknowledgment of finiteness prepares the leap into faith, hence only a God can save us) nor as the definitive assumption of the alternatives concretely presented by the situation. An ethics of finiteness is one that strives to keep faith with the discovery of the always insuperably finite situatedness of one's own provenance, while not forgetting the pluralistic implications of this discovery. In church I'm a saint, and in the tavern I'm one of the lads (an Italian motto that turns on the rhyme between *santi* and *fanti*), and I can never delude myself that I have found a stable perch somewhere that affords an all-encompassing view. Even as I utter the philosophical discourse you are reading, I'm only in another condition, which like any other imposes on me certain commitments: the particular condition of the philosopher, essayist, critic, never that of Universal Man. What ethics, what maxims of action, what rankings of values can I extract from this awareness (very rare even in the disenchanted philosophy of today: one notes the popularity of phenomenology or the tilt of philosophy toward the cognitive sciences)?

First of all, certainly, maxims and behaviors that display critical reserve. "If someone comes and says, behold the Messiah, don't believe it." Even the Messiah is mainly (and perhaps exclusively) present in the negative form of a critical ideal. So take a step back and lend a hand in the work, which is already underway, of nihilism. In every area of our existence, politics above all, we are faced with the duty of clearing away a forest of metaphysical absolutes, some of them long-established species, others invasive predators, like the laws of the market. Then: ever-renewed attention to the contents of our heritage and provenance. To avoid exaggerating the dimension of the past, we could even include all this in the category of alterity: obviously the voice of the other, our contemporary, toward whom we are responsible, is also provenance. This heeding will entail a quantity of philological choices, as when a scholar prepares a critical edition of a text: what to actively include and what to expunge from the core of ideas, values, principles, of which we consider ourselves the heirs and by which we feel ourselves summoned; a core to be defined through acts of responsible interpretive recognition. It is also work for professional intellectuals, but not exclusively, since in today's society, with the media spreading the content of the traditional culture of the West everywhere, and by now that of other cultures too, it is unthinkable that the work of heeding provenance (as Heidegger would call it) or of deconstruction (Derrida's well-known term) is a matter for a handful of professionals. To put it another way, in Nietzschean terms: he who doesn't become a superman today, which just means someone capable of interpreting for himself, is destined to perish—to perish as a free individual, at any rate. To delude oneself that there is a core of knowledge proper to natural man, accessible to anyone with sound common sense, is an error that is by now almost impossible to commit in good faith. The Church, the Churches? They cling tightly to the idea of a natural metaphysics accessible to the sound human intellect (guided, though, by the authoritative teaching of popes and priests: original sin does exist and in nonmythical language is called historicity), possibly out of skepticism about the possibility of making everyone into supermen and interpreters. But such skepticism (let us concede this much to the Enlightenment) is also the main thing keeping the possibility so remote.

The heeding of our heritage does not, therefore, lead only to the devaluation of all values but also to the reprise and continuation of certain inherited contents. Many rules of the game by which we know that our society lives will not simply be suspended or revoked in an ethic of finiteness. Many of them are ones that metaphysics or ecclesiastical authoritarianism have passed off as natural norms. Seen for what they are, a cultural inheritance rather than natures and essences, they can still hold good for us, but with a different cogency—as rational norms (acknowledged through a *dis-cursus*, a *logos*, through reason that reconstructs their self-constitution) liberated from the violence that characterizes ultimate principles and the authorities who see themselves as their keepers. Whether they still hold good or not is something that is decided in the name of whatever, with a responsible interpretation, we assume as characteristic of that which really belongs to the heritage to which we feel a commitment. Let us suppose that we are guided in this by nihilism, by the dissolution of ultimate foundations violently imposed through the silencing of dissent. The choice will then lie between what holds good and what doesn't in the cultural heritage from which we come. It will be made on the criterion of the reduction of violence and in the name of a rationality understood as discourse-dialogue between finite positions that acknowledge themselves as such and are therefore not tempted to override others on account of a legitimacy warranted by a first principle.

The overall meaning of this ethic of finiteness is the exclusion of the violence that sees itself as legitimate and the end of any violent authoritarian silencing of any interlocutor's questioning in the name of first principles. (Is there any other possible definition of violence that escapes the coils of essentialism?) As I have noted, this ethic certainly inherits, as for that matter do many philosophical ethics today, some aspects of Kantianism, specifically the formulation of the categorical imperative in terms of respect for the other (always consider the humanity in yourself and in others as an end, never simply as a means), but stripped of any dogmatic residues of the kind still detectable in the theory of communicative action of Habermas and the thought of Apel. In the ethic of finiteness, respect for the other is not even remotely grounded on the premise that he or she is a bearer of human reason equal in all men and women. From that position descends, in the neo-Kantian positions mentioned, the pedagogical-authoritarian implication that one does indeed heed the reasons of the other, but only on the prior stipulation that they have not been manipulated. Respect for the other is above all acknowledgment of the finiteness that characterizes each of us and that excludes any definitive effacement of the opacity that everyone bears inside himself or herself. It may be added that there are no positive reasons grounding this respect, itself indefinite: not, for example, acceptance that we are essentially equal, that we are all descendants of Adam, that my life depends on others, and so on. As soon as they are explicitly stated, these justifications reveal their vagueness and unsustainability. Only a familial prejudice could justify the command to love one's brothers, or a speciesist egoism the notion that I have to respect the other because he is made like me, or egoism pure and simple in the case where one is commanded to respect the other because one's own survival depends on him, and so on.

If, in assuming the nihilistic destiny of our epoch, we recognize that we have no ultimate foundation at our disposal, any possible legitimation for prevarication and violence toward others vanishes. Violence may always constitute a temptation, no more and no less than in any other ethical perspective, but with the difference that here this temptation is stripped of any semblance of legitimacy—which it isn't in essentialist ethics, even disguised ones (and that includes communicative ethics à la Habermas).

But if the guideline of the dissolution of principles and the reduction of violence is not demonstrated but assumed interpretively (therefore, always on the basis of arguments that are always rhetorical, verisimilar, etc.), does that mean that this ethic of finiteness is merely exhortation? Even a metaphysician like Aristotle recognized that the cogency of a mathematical demonstration is not the same thing as the persuasiveness of ethical discourses. If Hume's law is valid in some sense, ethics cannot speak in demonstrative terms. And Hume's law is the very condition of ethics, which can command, exhort, and judge only if that which must be done is not (a) fact.

PHILOSOPHY AND EMANCIPATION

To the consequences of the crisis of world communism and the oblivion into which Marx has fallen, we may add the loss of faith in the emancipatory power of philosophy, its capacity to produce practical effects on the individual and collective life of humanity. On the basis that Marx has been proved wrong, because of the failure of communist revolutions in the Soviet Union, China, and more recently Cuba, the famous eleventh proposition from his *Theses on Feuerbach* has also been discarded—the one that summons philosophy not to limit itself to interpreting the world but to set about changing it. I think that the state of (perpetual) war in which we find ourselves today also has roots, and not such unimportant ones, in the renunciation on the part of philosophy of its historical and political responsibility. When the arms of criticism no longer command attention from public opinion and politicians, then, to quote Marx again, it is the criticism of arms that takes over. I don't want to exaggerate the importance of the philosophy factor in international relations, but one may at least point out that the wars in Afghanistan and Iraq were launched in a trice and at the behest of a country in which philosophy has gradually been reduced to an academic function, an affair of specialists discussing problems of logic and epistemology in the leafy shelter of their university departments, virtually cut off from public opinion. This is not to challenge the other, and more familiar, perspective that sees violence ("terrorist," as it is labeled) and war as driven by religious faith (Muslim on one side, Christian

THE END OF PHILOSOPHY

fundamentalist on the other). The religious factor is certainly a matter of beliefs and mentalities, but it is not exactly a philosophical matter in the critical sense of the term. Philosophy blames the practical and economic sway of technology and its offshoots in every area of human life for its reduction to a pure descriptive account of the human condition (witness the often tautological conclusions of phenomenology) or to being a pure handmaiden to the experimental sciences (witness logic and epistemology). The hard sciences, for their part, find it easy to dispense with the proffered help altogether, being quite capable of organizing themselves in full autonomy and with great efficacy.

That is why, in an effort to explore the possibilities of a philosophy that might lead to emancipatory results, the second proposition-guideline that I want to adduce, to accompany the eleventh thesis on Feuerbach, is the much more scandalous assertion by Heidegger that "science doesn't think." It is a scandal because it represents the main obstacle in all debates on the relations between contemporary philosophy (at any rate, philosophy that doesn't undergo reduction in either of the two senses that I mentioned) and the sciences. And the scandal depends, as frequently happens, on ignorance of the precise meaning of Heidegger's proposition, which is first and foremost rigorously Kantian. For it is in Kant that we find the primary root of this thesis: science knows phenomena, applying the a priori of reason, space, time, and categories; thought, for its part, has as its "object" the noumenon, which cannot properly speaking be known in the realm of the phenomenon, only thought. But as we know, it is at the level of the noumenon that the questions most decisive for our human existence and for knowledge of the world in general arise. What can I know? What ought I to do? What can I hope for? These three questions, which Kant considers fundamental for any human significance in philosophy, are in no way questions to which science can respond. Not even the first, strictly speaking, is a matter of cognizance; the *Critique of Pure Reason* is certainly not an objective discourse of the scientific kind. When philosophy sets itself the goal of becoming a rigorous science (the dream of Husserl, which he came to see as *ausgeträumt*, or dreamed out, but which nevertheless remains the ideal of much phenomenology, not to mention Anglo-American philosophy), it loses all capacity to answer Marx's call in the eleventh thesis on Feuerbach or the appeal of Heidegger to think, to exercise our capacity to heed Being and not let ourselves be confined by calculating reason.

Very well, some might say. Let us accept the appeal of Marx and Heidegger. But what then does it signify to think, if it doesn't equal knowledge that applies rigorous rules and utilizes well-founded methods? If we try to answer that question, bearing in mind the two thinkers I have just mentioned and assuming their basic closeness to one another (which there is good reason to do, though finding Marx in Heidegger's company may be a bit of a shock), we arrive at the third proposition that guides me in the present line of thought, and once again it comes from Heidegger: "thought is thought of Being," in both senses of the genitive. It thinks Being (in the objective sense), but it is also the thought that inheres in Being, in the subjective sense. The phrase occurs in the later Heidegger, the man who resumes his discourse after the Second World War with the *Letter on Humanism* (1946), which he wrote in response to a request from Jean Beaufret and which is also a reply to the humanistic existentialism of Jean-Paul Sartre. In this letter, as in many prior works of the 1930s, we find an expression of what Heidegger calls the *Kehre*, the turn in his thought. To be brief, during the 1930s, when the huge political blocs destined to clash in the Second World War were forming (communist Russia, Nazi Germany, capitalist America and its allies), Heidegger realizes that the vision of *Dasein* elaborated in his monumental work of 1927, *Being and Time*, suffers from a limitation of an existentialist or humanistic kind. The idea of the authenticity and inauthenticity of that which exists can no longer, in his view, be likened to the point of view of the individual. The fact is that the authenticity and inauthenticity of existence depend profoundly (that is, entirely) on the historical conditions in which we are living. It is not an accident that in the *Letter on Humanism* Heidegger cites Marx's name with a surprising degree of respect—this coming from a former Nazi rector of the University of Freiburg. Of course, he does not reject the existential analytic of *Being and Time*, but he does express a new awareness that the authenticity of existence is not so much a question of the individual subject as it is (much more) a question that relates to the historical condition, which he calls *geschichtlich-geschicklich*. My preferred translation for this is "historico-destinal" (*storico-destinale*, dependent on history and destiny), because it does not result from individual decisions that might change at one stroke, with our good or bad will. Heidegger is speaking here of the fact that, in order to realize another way of being in the world no longer immersed in inauthenticity (I simplify a bit), we must wait for Being to return to us in a new mode. On this Marx would not agree, not explicitly anyway. But if one thinks, for example, of the Sartre of the *Questions of Method* (1957), where he says that the truth of existentialism is a provisional truth whose place will be taken by the true mode of knowledge, Marxism, only after the revolution (once again I summarize and simplify), it becomes clearer how the two positions are not so far apart.

Both Marx and, in very different terms, Heidegger point us in the direction of a thought that thinks Being. For the former, we know more or less clearly what this entails: all of knowledge, including the scientific kind, is conditioned in capitalist society by a false consciousness that doesn't know itself as such; it is known through ideology. The task of critical thought, meaning philosophy that aims to change the world, is to bring ideology to the fore and critique it, not taking as evident that which seems evident within the frame of what bourgeois thought regards as shared and certain knowledge. As for Heidegger, thought thinks Being to the extent that it does not limit itself to thinking-knowing existent beings (*gli "essendo,"* entities, things in existence), which are the objects of everyday knowledge (and scientific knowledge) made accessible to us within an aperture (something not unlike the Kantian a priori) that projects a frame of visibility. This aperture or frame may also be designated a paradigm, in the sense made familiar by Thomas Kuhn. Things are given as entities or emerge into existence through satisfying the preliminary conditions delineated within this frame. A paradigm or a historical-destinal aperture of truth is constituted by an ensemble of preliminary knowledges, received by an ensemble of expectations (for example, we don't now expect to meet vampires, but a hundred years ago we might have) and an ensemble of rules for verifying or falsifying propositions. Without going into further detail about the notion of aperture of truth in Heidegger, it is easy to see the analogy with the Marxist notion of ideology. They both share the character of historicity, inasmuch as the stability of existent beings, of objects, of the (mathematical and experimental) sciences is not an attribute of the aperture of Being itself. Existent things are given as such only within the aperture. For that matter, Kant too, while believing that human reason is always the same, did not succeed in objectivizing the subject, which he called *paralogismus*. Being, therefore—which opens us to the possibility of any experience in the world and of ourselves—is not a stable structure like the Being of Parmenides, the immutable Being of the Platonic ideas, or the essences in Aristotle.

To think Being (or to critique ideology), says Heidegger, it is necessary not to come to a halt or let oneself be halted in the face of the simple presence of what is immediately given. But to think on past presence is not easy for either Marx or Heidegger. Their difficulty in doing so depends on a sort of original sin (not that Heidegger would use that term or think it was eternally present in mankind) of our civilization, of our aperture of Being. In our day-to-day lives we tend to forget Being; it gets eclipsed by beings with a lowercase *b*, existent things. We surrender to common opinion, to what in *Being and Time* is called the world of assent (*man sagt, man stirbt*, etc.). Common opinion, precisely because it is common, cannot see objects as anything more than objects, accessible to all, neutral—which they never truly are. In Heidegger there is no explanation to be found for this tendency to forget Being, to limit oneself to the presence of the present and the object. Readers of Marx and Nietzsche might propose that the oblivion of Being in favor of beings depends on conditions of domination. Objectivity, the fact that that which is true is that which is verified on the basis of received criteria, is always preferred by the dominant classes: it is on these criteria that they dominate; read Walter Benjamin's theses "On the Concept of History" (1940). And wherever there is a truth "given" once and for all, there is always also someone who knows it more completely and rigorously than the rest of us: the central committee, the pope, those possessed of wisdom, the authority of the old sages, the philosopher class in Plato's *Republic*.

I will not develop further this connection between objectivity and metaphysics (as Heidegger calls thought that forgets Being and sees only present beings and hence identifies truth with verified objectivity within a received and robust paradigm). I think it would be possible, maybe through Nietzsche, to force even the Heideggerian perspective to accommodate the view that the tendency to objectivistic metaphysics is the result of domination and that hence it is the ideology of the dominant classes. The fact is that even Heidegger, when he is developing his critique of objectivistic metaphysics, doesn't try to construct an idea of Being different from objectivism, a truer and more, so to speak, objective notion of Being, to set against it. He is much more concerned, like much of the rest of the intellectual avant-garde of the early twentieth century, to take a stand against positivistic objectivism allied to industrialization and the reduction of humanity to machinery, which Charlie Chaplin depicted in *Modern Times*.

The value of Heidegger is that he gives us the more acceptable legitimation of the goal of getting beyond metaphysics. Marx falls short here because he always criticizes ideology in the name of some truth. The proletariat's right to make the revolution is grounded, ultimately, on the fact that only the proletariat perceives the truth (of mankind and history—and of the economy too, with the results that we observed in the five-year-plans of Stalin and Mao) because, not having any interests of its own to obfuscate its gaze (only its muscle power and reproductive capacity), it sees as if from nowhere, realizes the true absolute knowledge of which Hegel dreamed. So this right of the proletariat is grounded in its capacity for truth, and that is a metaphysical stance. In effect, emancipation for Marx (what I call salvation) depends on objective knowledge of truth, unfiltered by ideology. And that is one of the sources, not the only one, for the tendency of real communism, Soviet and Chinese style, to evolve into authoritarian regimes. If the proletarian revolution has taken place, then we are now in the regime of truth, which needs to be protected against any heresy or demand for change. But if one can imagine Marx scrubbed free of these metaphysical residues, then it would be possible to imagine an ideal (as opposed to "real") communism able to withstand the Popperian attack on the Marxist philosophy of history, and in principle on Plato, as the enemies of the open society.

At this point of the discourse we find ourselves back where we began, with Marx's thesis on Feuerbach. What would it mean for philosophy to transform, or help to transform, the world and make it more desirable than, more rationally preferable to, the effectual condition into which we are *immer schon* (already always) thrown? The projectual character of any existence (which was the projectual result that Heidegger reached in *Being and Time*) can only become concrete in or through a historical project that, precisely because historical, is also inevitably political and collective. It is here perhaps, in this conclusion exposed to such high risk (a risk to which Heidegger fell victim by taking part in the Nazi revolution), that is to be found the only possible meaning of the famous thesis on authenticity as the foreseen decision to assume one's own death (*zum Tode sein*) or, rather, one's own mortality. We read somewhere in *Being and Time* that the way to avoid taking the past as *vergangen* (as irrevocable necessity, as the stony weight of *es war* that oppressed Nietzsche's Zarathustra) and instead assuming it as *gewesen* (a having-been ever open to our interpretation and decision) is for *Dasein* to select its heroes. To assume one's own mortality: an act about which *Being and Time* says nothing further, evidently so as to avoid lapsing into ontological moralism in light of Heidegger's *Kehre* of the 1930s, hence a concrete commitment within the effectual history of the historical community to which one belongs.

The content of the commitment is here marked by a sort of Kantian formalism. Heideggerian ontology doesn't supply guidance about which side to choose. But the very fact that it rejects the assumption of history as a *vergangen*, as an imposition that we can only submit to (the watchword of every variety of traditionalism and conservatism), puts the Heideggerian perspective closer to what, in brighter times than those we are living in now, was called permanent revolution. Heidegger himself failed to understand this when he opted for Hitler in 1933, spellbound by the notion that the premetaphysical past that he projected mythically onto preclassical Greece might be revived in Hitler's Germany. Still, on the basis of the results of the existential analytic and the *Kehre*, the path toward historical commitment was correctly traced out: *Dasein* did select its heroes, its historical models, to assert, again and afresh, the possibility of a nonpassive attitude to the past. The choice is and must be guided by the ideal of the overcoming of metaphysics, the overcoming of objectivity, the overcoming of the realism of political conservatism. The only thing that humanity should be doing in the world, as far as political conservatism is concerned, is observing it, in the double sense of knowing it objectively and submitting to its true structure, taken as the moral norm. Wrong, says Heidegger: even at the risk of adopting a mistaken position, one must assume the responsibility of a project. And this project will be more authentic the more it surrenders the claim to attain the truth once and for all, which would be to deny its own basic objective. From the viewpoint of the new revolutionary Heidegger that I am (re)presenting here, the basis of any historical project must be negation of the violence that is the heritage of metaphysics, negation of conservatism and domination under the pretexts of truth, the datum, order.

This is where it becomes decisively important for philosophy to reflect on the meaning of Heidegger's Nazi error. But not for the reason adduced periodically by scholars on a mission to eradicate the bad seed of his philosophical teaching, to wit that learning about what it leads to will inoculate our culture against the disease of Heideggerianism. It is important because, from the same premises that drove Heidegger and that he himself misunderstood when he joined the Hitler movement, it is possible to start over and imagine a philosophy responsive to Marx's demand, a philosophy able to modify the world through a historical initiative, not just observe it. The meaning of Heidegger's Nazi error lies not in his decision to choose his heroes and get himself involved in a political adventure. It doesn't even lie, and this point is essential, in the fact that he deserted truth and embraced a cause that was objectively the wrong one. Heidegger's critics have always found him culpable for never having acknowledged the mistake he had made after the war, and anyone with the slightest pretension to democratic ideals of civilized life can only concur with that wholeheartedly. Nobody wishes more than I do that Martin Heidegger had purged himself by disowning the positions he took in

1933. But could he really have done so on the basis that the (theoretical, ethical) truth had finally come to light? Because that is what the logic of Nuremberg seems to lead to. One condemns one's own (and others') Nazism in the name of the universal human rights that have finally become self-evident and been solemnly sworn to by the side that won the Second World War. I realize that this is treading on dangerous ground, what with all the historical revisionism about in many European countries, concomitant with the general and deplorable revival of the conservative right. The United States, even under the Bush presidency, has proved resistant to it, because Nazism features as one of the incarnations of evil in the popular imagination there, and it's a national duty to demonize it. But tread this ground I must, otherwise the claim to be speaking, acting, and deciding in the name of truth just keeps on serving as a cover for the logic of war.

So then: if not in the name of the metaphysical truth that Nazism was an inhuman monstrosity, in what terms could or should Heidegger have expressed a personal conversion after the war? This question he never explicitly addressed. But a weak reading of his ontology can help us to elicit an answer. Just as Being never gives itself in person (which seems an odd conclusion for a thinker who wanted to go "to things themselves"—one more sign of the need to move beyond phenomenology), so likewise the *Dasein* that chooses heroes for itself is always finite and situated. In 1933, Heidegger chose the "damned part," but so, albeit with different historical coordinates, did other great thinkers like Bloch and Lukács when they chose Stalinism. Ontological difference, which he had forgotten in 1933 by deluding himself that Hitler's Germany could become a revival of preclassical Greece, mythically imagined as a land where Being was still present, was

precisely what kept Heidegger from repeating the error of invest-
ing once more in the belief that the true truth had now, at last,
shone its light on him. So he maintained silence about the error or
sin he had committed, probably thinking that, in the altered circumstances, the only option left if he were not to pretend to stand
in the light of truth like the judges at Nuremberg was to remain
wordless and pursue his thinking about the mode of Being's
eventuation in our time. It's as though he were starting afresh
from where he had been in 1935 when he wrote his *Introduction to
Metaphysics*—as though the end of Nazism had somehow not happened. But then, that was Theodor Adorno's firm conviction too;
he saw Nazi totalitarianism as living on after death in the democratic world of advertising, propaganda, and goods for sale in
phantasmagoric plenty. So to get past, or through to the far side
of, his Nazi mistake appeared to Heidegger a good deal more
complicated than a simple recantation, an easy confession with
an easy penance, which is how the morality tale being performed
in public always struck him. It is hard to say if we still have anything to learn from Heidegger about the whole business. But at
bottom we are still where he was in 1935, even if we have no reser-
vations about the judgments passed at Nuremberg, which we obviously endorse. But not in the name of Truth. Rather as a matter
of keeping faith with our determinate historical situation: it is
our duty to resist the temptation to feel ourselves allied with
Truth—like the exponents of terrorism by whom we are beset today, from Bush exporting democracy with bombs to the Bin
Laden brigade trying to impose Sharia law on the whole world.
We know we are historically finite and therefore always exposed
in politics to the risk of choosing with partiality, but that gets cor-
rected for in the course of negotiating with others, individuals or

groups, just as partial and finite as we are. Perhaps one thing that philosophy can do to start transforming the world instead of just contemplating it is to teach us that we are always party—party to negotiation, party to dialogue, and party to conflict, which we can try to regulate with norms and tribunals but can't eliminate.

Today especially, when the world appears increasingly divided between terroristic dogmas claiming to represent truth, (infinite?) justice, and definitive human authenticity (be it formal democracy Western style or the ideal of governing in conformity with divine Sharia law), Heidegger's heritage remains available and has much to teach us.

DIALECTIC, DIALOGUE, AND DOMINATION

Philosophy is always ahead of its time. Nietzsche felt himself eminently untimely, but the same holds good for other philosophers too, ones whom we still regard with good reason as our contemporaries. Take the example of the philosophers of poststructuralism. Their goal of "upending Platonism" has never seemed as topical to me as it does today, but at the time, forty years ago, it looked like rhetorical exaggeration. The reason why the anti-Platonism of Deleuze, Derrida (with his defense of writing against the myth of Thoth), Lyotard, and Foucault is topical is this: the authoritarian reaction of metaphysics as it struggles against its own dissolution has become increasingly plain for all to see and, on that account, intolerable. Take for example the notions of dialogue, or democracy, that in the 1960s and 1970s were still utilized and respected; today they are ideological avatars, objects of suspicion on sight—and not just at the academic or high-culture level. In a culture that talks all the time about dialogue, no one really believes that dialogue offers a way to solve the problems we face of relations among different individuals, groups, and cultures. Those who still subscribe to this rhetoric are late-blooming Platonists, metaphysicians who have deep faith in the objectivity of (their) truth and who live in hope of seeing it triumph in the wake of an exchange of views untainted by interests, passions, and ignorance; an exchange that in the end is perspicuous rather than opaque. Platonism doesn't just happen to be a dialogic philosophy by chance: faith in a truth that those who strive with good will and under expert guidance will always come to intuit is the precondition that makes dialogue productive. That is why the individual who steers things along in many Platonic dialogues, the helmsman if you like, is Socrates: the philosopher whom Nietzsche portrayed as having killed off tragedy by imposing the conviction that the world is a rational order and that the (morally and theoretically) just have nothing to fear. In Platonic dialogue, with its grounding in faith in a rational order of the world, you can even discern the same schema that undergirds Aristotle's *Poetics*, which Bertolt Brecht criticized as the optimism of winners: all the sufferings of Oedipus turn out to be justified in the end, and the spectator's task comes down to *pathei mathos*, learning the lessons that suffering teaches. It's only an analogy, but it does cast some light on the sovereignist spirit that drives both Plato in his dialogic practice and Aristotle in his analysis of tragedy.

The question is the one already posed by Nietzsche in his critique of Socratism: is the order of the world that guarantees a correct outcome of the dialogue and that justifies tragedy (even against the criticism of Plato in *The Republic*, book 10) truly a just, rational, universally valid order? In any case, it is the postulate guaranteeing the value of the Platonic method. Here Nietzsche is not objecting against Socrates that the rationality of his vision of the world is false, as though it were a theory that, properly modified, would yield a different truth. Nietzsche is not addressing the theoretical verity or falsity of the Socratic creed. He is registering, or "constatating" in philosophical parlance, that this creed kills tragedy, meaning that its practical upshot is "quietive" (a word that Schopenhauer employed to highlight the contrast with "motive"). A bit like the injunction *pathei mathos*, the Socratic theory creates a consciousness half content and half wearily resigned: the world goes how it goes, so (in demotic American English) suck it up.

One oughtn't exaggerate the practical implications either of Platonic dialogue or the Aristotelian doctrine of tragedy. But it isn't far-fetched to observe that the latter especially has a component of resigned acceptance that is halfway to submission. Is the *eureka* of the slave who discovers a geometrical theorem for himself really a cry of joy,[2] or is it the expression of a more ambivalent state of mind? Do I perhaps show excessive sensitivity to the elements of domination entailed by the structure of dialogue, which have never aroused similar suspicions over all the centuries during which the Platonic dialogue has been taken as the model of rational argumentation *par excellence*? What accounts for this new sensitivity and the spirit of suspicion it seems to betray? As I said, the anti-Platonism of authors like Deleuze and Lyotard has become topical again in our culture, because the end of metaphysics, of which they too speak in a manner more or less explicitly derived from Heidegger and Nietzsche, has reached an acute phase characterized by ever more explicit and violent defensive postures. So it is worth repeating that, in referring to metaphysics, we are not talking only about a discipline but also about an epoch in the history of Being in the Heideggerian sense of the expression. In Heideggerian language, metaphysics equals the identification of Being with the existent being, the entity. In Parmenides and Plato, true Being was the attribute of the eternal ideas, given to the intellect as pure forms.

The course of Western philosophy and culture (and that includes material culture) has made this order ever more real. It is instantiated in the society of total organization made possible by science and its technological applications. Metaphysics, the rational order in which every entity is fitted securely into the chain of cause and effect, reaches its end at the moment at which it reveals itself to be intolerable—precisely because fully realized. European colonialism and imperialism were the modalities through which metaphysics became the order of the world. And an example of refusal to tolerate this world was the revolt of the colonialized peoples, who were no longer prepared to stand for being exploited as though they were subhuman primitives needing to be introduced into the world by us, their masters. It's a well-known story. But what is happening is that the masters, now no longer colonial states but the new conglomerations of global economic power that have taken their place, are refusing to abandon their dominant position. The ideological screen isn't concealing the struggle so well; it's becoming more explicit: the cold war of the 1950s has become hot war in many of the world's regions, with the values at stake ever more self-evidently material, for example, energy resources. Nietzsche called the increasingly brazen, violent, and elementary capitalist competition of his time *sauvagerie indienne* (a reference to what was then the stereotype of the American Indian or rather the Wild West in general). Thus it is that in the world of the end of metaphysics, it becomes impossible to speak of truth. "There do not exist facts, only interpretations; and if this too is an interpretation, so be it." This Nietzschean aphorism is evidently not a description of some reality "out there." But it was made possible exactly because the unity of truth (and of the order of the world) has become unpronounceable: it is just not sayable any longer. Those whom it excludes would revolt, and it's a fight they would win. In the new condition of the world at the end of metaphysics, what is occurring with respect to dialogue is turning Platonism upside down in this sense: what counts is no longer the hope of finding truth at the conclusion of the debate but rather the very fact that debate is possible and that it should continue, as Rorty says. Take the example of interreligious dialogue. Are we supposed to expect the result of this dialogue to be conclusions about God, man, and morality formulated in terms acceptable to all? The theologians and Church leaders who attend may decide to issue a concluding statement to the press, but it will only deal in generalities and common, human (all-too-human?) sense, nothing specifically religious. The fact is that the goal of interreligious dialogue (or a dialogue on values, ethics, the meaning of existence) is just the dialogue itself. It is not a process that lets us derive values because it allows us to discover a truth on which we agree. All it does is allow us to realize ourselves through discussion and conversation, excluding violent struggle.

Some may ask: Is there nothing more to it than that? I might answer, in the words of Hölderlin, that man has nominated many gods from the moment that we are a dialogue. If we take the poet at his word, mankind has not nominated *a* truth or *a* God but various truths and various gods. I don't know whether this corresponds to the poet's intention; he always uses the plural "gods," and Jesus was only the last of them, but it is safe to say that to his mind dialogue does not give rise to convergence on a single unifying truth. Upending Platonism means, among other things, assigning a different (and even, I daresay, dif-ferent) function to dialogue. Where dialogue is the search for a unique truth, it always generates the conflictual drive, the struggle for domination. But let us concede as well that dialogue does promote conflict avoidance, in the sense that to probe for opportunities for dialogue inevitably generates, or evokes, the need to be done for good with violent struggle and domination. So a complex dialectic arises between conflict and dialogue, which at least explains why all the talk about the need for dialogue that we hear these days sounds so empty and hypocritical. It's because the phase of struggle and conflict has to precede the onset of dialogue. Who could imagine a constitution being founded simply by citizens voting on a referendum? Without rules in place, in other words a constitution, there is no such thing as a referendum. The question of dialogue and conflict always brings us back to face the question of violence. There is no escape from the struggle between master and servant, wonderfully described in Hegel's *Phenomenology of Spirit*. It is an illusion, dangerous because entirely aimed at preserving the current balance of power, to imagine replacing conflict with dialogue. Conflict is needed to establish the conditions for dialogue. Knowing that is a barrier against falling for the ideological illusions that power always employs to preserve itself. But knowing that conflict is necessary in order for dialogue to commence also constitutes the normative limit of every liberation struggle. The essential motivation of the struggle for liberation is the effort to give a voice to those who didn't have one before, as Walter Benjamin wrote. For Benjamin too, the meaning of dialogue is primarily the very fact of beginning it. And this confers a somewhat ironic meaning on philosophical theories of nonopaque communication, the only kind seen as capable of guaranteeing the foundations of human society. The question may also be discerned, in more radical but starker terms, in Giambattista Vico's opposition to Thomas Hobbes and his theory of the social contract. Vico objected against Hobbes that the original social contract could only be stipulated if there were already a language and a code of communication in place: precisely the things that make the contract itself possible.

This observation does not necessarily mean that philosophy must give way before the necessity of violence. Rather, it is a matter of not ignoring, in any theory, this foundational phase that entails an initiative of emancipation that can only be called revolutionary. Hobbes's defense is that his idea of the contract concerns only the remote origins of any society. We never experience an absolute origin of society, because we always find ourselves in conditions established prior to us. Does this allow us to forget all about the problem of original violence? It is a violence that is revived every time that dialogue turns into a pure and simple pedagogical expedient of the Platonic kind. The struggle against metaphysics, says Heidegger, is never conclusively won. Any evocation of dialogue as a human approach to the solution of social conflicts must also contain an explicit theory of the conflict that always accompanies the instauration or restoration of dialogic conditions. There never exists a normal constitutional situation. Those who invite us to behave as though it were already in place are doing no more than expressing the ideology of the groups currently in power. Theory can, at least, refrain from upholding this equivocation and help to render it less burdensome.

CONVERSION AND CATASTROPHE

Stasis has gripped the world religions to the point where it is hard to imagine what a real conversion would be like anymore. Would anyone still feel impelled to convert from Catholicism to Calvinism, for example, or vice versa? Even if a Catholic decides to convert to Buddhism or Hinduism, it requires no special transformation of her own beliefs or customs, only an addition to, or a slight modification of, her vision of life. The principle of dialogue excludes the very possibility of a dramatic change. Yet no more than fifty years ago in Catholic Italy, a great secular intellectual (Curzio Malaparte, in the case in point) could provoke scandal and public uproar simply by requesting the sacraments of confession and communion on his deathbed. In more recent years, on the other hand, and not always for purely electoral reasons, many communist politicians have identified as believing Catholics. I remember that Federico Fellini was one of those attended by a priest, a cardinal in fact, as he lay dying. Fellini is a good example of the kind of person who doesn't invest too heavily in the belief system but isn't a priest-hater either. Many of his films, especially *La Dolce Vita*, are expressions of this sort of Italian Catholic attitude. But there is nothing specifically Italian about aversion to conversion. Take, for example, the relatively uniform political atmosphere in the countries of the European Union. It isn't just Italy in which it is increasingly difficult to distinguish between the political platforms and actions of the left and the right. The fall of the

Berlin Wall even stripped the communist world of its alterity. Putin is a good personal friend of Silvio Berlusconi, who always swore he would never be friends with a communist or ex-communist. Someone may ask: what about al-Qaeda? This question naturally opens up the whole problem of Islam, which seems more profoundly different and not so easily neutralizable. We know that in Islam conversion to another religion is punishable by the death penalty. Yet I wonder if it is really valid to bring that particular case into a discussion of conversion. No one, even a seriously believing Christian, would counsel a Muslim to convert at the cost of his life. In many respects, the risk of conversion is linked to its political and public aspect but in no sense to the religious and salvific significance of the act. Thus conversion becomes a political act. In general today, the division between Muslims and Christians is primarily or exclusively a question of belonging to one side rather than the other. It is noteworthy that this political and public significance of conversion is profoundly rooted in the very history of European Christianity. After the individual conversions of apostolic times, the conversions of entire peoples of Europe to Christianity were determined by the conversion of their sovereign—which was not necessarily, on his part, a personal conversion to the faith.

My point of view is that today it is very difficult to talk about conversion in the "catastrophic" sense that my subtitle suggests. For one thing, there is the growing spiritualization of religiosity, which brings it about that even priests and official representatives of the faiths no longer attribute great importance to the external signs of membership in a Church (which for Catholics raises the question of the significance of the sacraments). For another, there is the generally pacifist attitude of contemporary society, which tends to confine warfare to the periphery of the developed world. Or to the war on terrorism, which expands the definition of crime to include any form of practical dissent that perturbs the established legal order. To adapt an expression from Nietzsche, we are no longer "material for conversion." Or, to borrow a term from another no less suspect author, Carl Schmitt, we (the citizens of the developed First World) are living in a general atmosphere of *Neutralisierung*, neutralization. This may be because of the unchallenged dominance of the American empire, which no longer has a rival in the Soviet Union and doesn't yet have one in India or China, or because of the fact that our general problems only have a narrow range of possible solutions, with ecology and survival imposing a sort of technical constraint on all our options. Terrorism and local crime only serve to camouflage these basic problems. They are, if you like, a stratagem for consoling us, in the face of that which threatens the very possibility of life on the planet. The question is: is there not a consolatory significance in our talking about conversion and catastrophe? We feign belief that something might really happen, something that would amount to a transformation or even a transfiguration. But nothing does happen, and maybe nothing like that can happen, because if it did there would probably be no continuation, there would be no new world in which we would be able to enjoy a new life. We are not summoned to follow our Messiah to Mount Tabor, and even if we were, we would be unable to take up residence there. I don't know if this situation corresponds to the end of history in Fukuyama's sense, especially since things continue to go along, and what seems to be excluded is only and precisely what we most desire: conversion, catastrophe, revolution.

So what the heading above suggests is that the experience of conclusion that we are living through in our time, both at the level of political action and that of theoretical projects (for example the decline of utopian thought), is a symptom of the end of metaphysics. Metaphysics, as we have seen, ends with the universal domination of technology, realizing the metaphysical dream of the universal organization of all beings within an ever more predictable structure of cause and effect. We haven't yet come to the point where the dream is totally realized, of course; you could say that the long goodbye of the God who died in Nietzsche is still going on. But broadly speaking, the scientific-technological order is already reality, especially in social and political terms. What does seem ever more impossible in our world is a radical change, even one of local dimensions like the French Revolution, never mind the Russian Revolution of 1917. Heidegger calls the technological order in which we live the *Gestell*. His English translator, Joan Stambaugh, once translated it with "framework," and that reminds me of an expression familiar from crime thrillers that also conveys the philosophical point neatly: "we've been framed." We have been caught, trapped, enmeshed in a nexus from which there is no exit.[3]

I am well aware that not everyone may have been framed yet, that I am leaving out of consideration peoples and individuals who haven't been fitted into the framework, especially in the so-called Third World. (The Second World, Russia and China and so on, is by now totally absorbed into the Western economic system.) Herbert Marcuse's old idea that the revolutionary proletariat of our time is to be sought in the masses of the Third World finds an echo here. Indeed, virtually the only place where political innovation is occurring at present is in parts of the Third World that have found the strength to resist American imperialism: Cuba, Venezuela, and Bolivia. But not even these alternative realities appear to be the heralds of an authentic revolution of the kind imagined by Marx. We cannot expect a radical mutation in class relations, if we ever could. Paradoxically, the more the masses are involved in political processes, the less it is possible to envision radical change. The interests of the large masses are clearly comprehensible if we consider the policies of trade unions. The unions can fight hard against the dominant economic power, but at the end of every strike there still has to be an improvement in the circumstances of the working classes. The unions can never be revolutionary agents; they are compelled to act within the political and economic system, protecting it against a general collapse. Has there ever been a popular revolution? The French Revolution doesn't fit that bill, nor the Soviet one. We must face up to the mythological character of the very idea of radical change. It expresses the need for change in terms of conversion and catastrophe, which are indeed kinds of radical change. But the need is more ideological than realistic. Can we posit that conversion, like revolution, is always, within certain limits, a myth? Naturally we take for granted that on the road to Damascus, Paul had a conversion experience. But any account we have of it is far from first hand, transmitted to us in mythological texts. One thinks of the lines from Hölderlin: "Nur zu Zeiten ertraegt goettliche Fuelle der Mensch / Traum von Ihnen is drauf das Leben" (only at intervals does man bear divine fullness. Dream of them is, after, life).

Can we state that today the very idea of a radical and profound transformation in our personal lives and, more than that, in society is no longer thinkable? And that this is probably not just a condition specific to recent modernity but an indication of the mythical and ideological character of the idea of revolution? When I ponder these questions, I think not only of Hölderlin but Sartre as well, specifically his *Critique of Dialectical Reason*. For him there is only one authentic moment of revolution, the moment when the group "fuses," has a momentary experience of *goettliche Fuelle*. It soon gives way to the reconstitution of bureaucratic distinctions and the rise of a new dominant class. It is hard to say whether Heidegger, in his thinking on the end of metaphysics and the problem of surpassing it, also had these questions in mind. While it may not be possible to attribute interests of this sort to him, it remains the case that what we have in mind when we talk about the end of metaphysics includes the general social and political condition of his and our world. Very probably, after his unfortunate adventure with Hitler and Nazism, he no longer wished to associate his philosophy with political situations and so avoided going in the direction in which I am going here. But purely on the basis of his texts, it is highly reasonable to propose an interpretation of the notion of *Verwindung*—distortion, acceptance, resignation—that takes into account its political, social, and even psychological implications.

Let me sum up the main lines of what I propose. From the start, the idea of citing conversion and catastrophe in the heading is an expression of the need for radical change and the awareness of how problematic the possibility of it is. My opinion is that any such possibility is linked to the accelerating unification of the contemporary world under the parallel impacts of imperialism, economic globalization, and technology. All these factors are responsible for the absence of an authentic event in our world. This absence of event finds expression not just in Heidegger's philosophy, where Being is *Ereignis*, event, but also in thinkers like Levinas and Derrida, who reach toward alterity, toward the new and the unexpected, or in Richard Rorty's conceptual clarification of hermeneutics in terms of Thomas Kuhn's abnormal science.

Heidegger's concept of the end of metaphysics may also, however, point us toward ways of escape from this condition of finality. Of this Heidegger was aware, having found out the hard way while trying to finish *Sein und Zeit* (or so he says, at any rate, in the *Letter on Humanism*) that metaphysics cannot be surpassed—in our terms, that revolution/conversion is not possible. The only way out of or past the domination of metaphysics available to us is what he calls *Verwindung*. He invests this everyday German word with a special meaning, as a practicable alternative to *Überwindung*, which would mean overcoming or surpassing. If we ponder our own current situation in light of Heidegger's *Verwindung*, both the meaning of our world and what it would mean to change it in some manner appear in a different light. For one thing, and this was decisive for Heidegger himself, we will no longer regard conversion and radical transformation as matters of individual choice. This is why the word *Eigentlichkeit*, "authenticity," disappears from Heidegger's texts, its place taken by *Ereignis*, "event," which, significantly, has the same etymological root (*eigen*). The *Kehre*, the turn of the 1930s, leads Heidegger away from his original existentialistic stance toward the more explicitly ontological positions of the later works. Conversion is a question regarding Being as such, not our individual relations with beings. This is, in the end, my reason for explicitly linking the themes of conversion and catastrophe to the concept of the (possibility or impossibility of) revolution. From a philosophical perspective, such a change has to do with the end of metaphysics in the sense that it is exactly in the world of the end of metaphysics (the *Gestell* or pervasive domination of technological rationalization) that man and the world lose the traits conferred upon them by metaphysics, in other words the character of subject and object (see Heidegger 1957). A great deal of what sociologists and social psychologists describe fits into the categories outlined by Heidegger here, starting with the feeling of the absence of authentic event. The developed world, where metaphysics is at its end, displays a worrying lack of projectuality, except for the effort to maintain the present way of life, with its privileges and habits of consumption. The war on terrorism is just part of that effort. Then there is the Third World, dominated by the same model, trying to achieve the same level of well-being and consumption that the West has exported everywhere. *Plus ça change, plus c'est la même chose* seems to be the motto of history now. The difficulty experienced by Heidegger in his effort to surpass metaphysics is also the meaning of our experience of the impossible dream of conversion.

So what about the chances of escaping metaphysics, if not through an *Überwindung* then at least through a movement of *Verwindung*? Does it offer a real way out, or will it amount to no more than a subjectivistic stance of ironic and unsullied detachment toward the existing political, economic, and technological-metaphysical order? Can we ultimately expect some sort of conversion that won't just wear the features of ironic acceptance of the world the way it is? As I have noted, *Verwindung* is a common word basically meaning convalescence, the fact of continuing to bear the marks of a disease of which one has been cured. Seen in that light, *Verwindung* does seem to be the mark of a purely passive attitude, a sort of ontological fatalism that brings to mind the moment of Stoicism and skepticism in Hegel's *Phenomenology of Spirit*. But I would prefer to draw attention to another implication of the word: the prefix *ver-* does allude, however vaguely, to a distortion, a change of direction of movement, a slight diversion rather than some radical change. The importance of *Verwindung* as a concept lies entirely in this allusion to change that does seem feasible, instead of overcoming and revolution, precisely because it does not include the force and violence of a general upheaval of the type Nietzsche had in mind when he spoke of an *Umwertung aller Werte*, a revaluation of all values. Is this shift so light and noiseless that it is just an inner, spiritual change? When he chose Hitler's party in 1933, Heidegger was not thinking of a purely intimate conversion. He made a commitment, wrongly of course, to a historical and political effort to transform Germany, Europe, and perhaps the world. The idea of *Verwindung* appears only some time later in his work (see Heidegger 1954) and is clearly in part a way of taking his distance from his political error of 1933 (which for that matter was also a self-misunderstanding of his own notion of ontological difference, since it implied that Being, in its presumably premetaphysical *Anwesen*, might again be experienced as fully present). That notwithstanding, it is the case that Heidegger was uninterested in change of a purely theoretical and philosophical kind, so that a political reading of his concept of *Verwindung* is not a betrayal of his underlying intentions. Hence: no revolution, no overcoming, either political or spiritual, but a *Verwindung*, and not just for philosophers but for all of us, for the world. Philosophy's claim to universality is not surrendered in the least; that would be to betray its task. It would make no sense to propose *Verwindung* as a way of escape from metaphysics if we were to conceive philosophy as just a special form of knowledge, one science among others, an academic discipline. In fact, even this mode of viewing philosophy, the mode well represented by someone like John Searle, for example, does entail a commitment with respect to the general order of the world, by which I mean a commitment to true and proper order, to an ordered division of labor within which philosophical theory has its assigned place and task. Serious labor within the true and proper order of the scientific disciplines is a mode from which any need for conversion is excluded from the start—in fact prior to the start. That is a mode that Husserl even at his most scientific would not accept, for he viewed the philosopher as a sort of "professional of the human condition."

Husserl, and for that matter the entire philosophical tradition, conceived philosophy as conversion/revolution in the sense that I am trying to illuminate. The novelty of Heidegger's *Verwindung* is that he, like Marx, does not believe in a purely interior form of conversion but comprehends in the notion the general condition of the world, which he calls *Gestell* and which Marx called capitalist society. And, unlike Marx, Heidegger considers that conversion/revolution is no longer possible in the world of the end of metaphysics. The only thing left for us is *Verwindung*.

Let me attempt a provisional conclusion by discussing what *Verwindung* might mean, as something more than the purely spiritual and subjective stance of a philosopher or public intellectual in the current situation. The sole examples to be found in recent philosophical literature are, in my view, Derrida's conception of deconstruction and the principle of anarchy that animate Reiner Schürmann's book. If he is to take seriously the task of conversion, the public intellectual, the philosopher, cannot limit himself to the practice of purely textual deconstruction, which most American followers of Derrida do. Nor can she think anarchy in the same theoretical vein, practicing deconstruction as a way of distancing herself—genealogically, historically—from all the first principles that customarily dominated the metanarrative of the metaphysical tradition. A philosopher must convert in the sense that he cannot do otherwise than attempt to be in practical contact with all the phenomena of practical deconstruction of the still metaphysical order of his and our society. The latter cannot be radically overcome (no revolution of the world proletariat would have any chance of success within the real relations of power), but it can certainly be "*verwunden*-distorted" by the multiple anarchic initiatives of resistance springing up here and there within the *Gestell*, even without any (metaphysical) hope of constructing a new global order (another *ausgetraümt* dream of traditional philosophy). This is perhaps the only possible conversion that we can attempt to bring about.

WHY HEGEL NOW?

This heading is not original, but it may usefully be borrowed from Richard J. Bernstein and paired with a 1965 essay by Gadamer on the "Philosophical Foundations of the Twentieth Century" (Bernstein 1977 and Gadamer 1965). The latter is one of the most illuminating for understanding the specific Hegelianism of the master of twentieth-century hermeneutics, and it made a striking impression on me because it proposes a reading of Hegel (affirming that we must follow Hegel only as far as the objective spirit) extraordinarily close (albeit independent and linked rather to Dilthey) to the reform of Hegelian dialectic that constituted the program of Benedetto Croce early in the twentieth century. These references, especially the one to Bernstein, a neopragmatist American thinker, demarcate the terrain on which I intend to offer an updated response to the question he put thirty years ago. He was thinking more in historical than programmatic terms, but my proposed answer reverses that order of priority. Bernstein asked why, in the North American philosophical environment of the time, with the crisis of neopositivism well under way and epistemology still the dominant orientation in departments of philosophy, there should nevertheless be a revival of interest in Hegel.[4] It was a provocative but strictly theoretical question, whereas I ask myself why it appears as though, in the current philosophical situation, Hegel has something important to say, quite apart from his status as a classic and the object of continuing research by historians of philosophy. But I shall refrain from also discussing Croce's famous essay of 1906, "Quel che è vivo e quel che è morto nella filosofia di Hegel" ("What Still Lives and What Is Dead in Hegel's Philosophy"), because for one thing it seems to me that Croce doesn't really regard any aspect of Hegel's thought as dead. And precisely on account of the "neopragmatist" inspiration that I adopt here (not really so distant from Croce), I would never dream of declaring anything living or dead—only actual or less actual in a given cultural situation, or, in Heidegger's terms, a given "epoch of Being."

But while I avoid the hubris of issuing certificates of life and death, I may be guilty of another kind, which is typical of all thought that attempts to get away from absolutist metaphysics and open itself to historicity, to the event. I declare Hegel "actual" (of importance right now) in relation to a philosophical situation that I believe I can summarize in a few traits. What happens here is a bit the same as what happens when one discusses modernity and the postmodern: real historians always object that neither modernity nor, ex fortiori, postmodernity is an object definable and summarizable in rigorous terms. Such an observation derives from, and leads straight back to, a metaphysical and essentialist position from which, if I decide to address a specific philosophical theme, I can justify my choice only with reference to its eternal urgency in the order of essences, certainly not with reference to pressures that I read in the present situation. I recall here in passing that one of the constant debates that I had for many years with the late Jacques Derrida, a great master and a friend, revolved around the fact that, after his inaugural text *Of Grammatology* (1967), in which he speaks of the urgency of his theme for the present, he never again wrote a proem of this historical-situational kind. Indeed, he displayed an increasing preference for a more ahistorical stance. In Richard Rorty's terms, to which I shall return, we would say that Derrida accentuated his filiation with the Kantian strain of modern philosophy as against what Rorty called the Hegelian strain.

Allow me to state, with all the veneration that I felt and feel for Derrida, that my own preference for the Hegelian and historicist (or hermeneutic and Heideggerian) lineage is driven more by ethical than by simply theoretical considerations. I am interested, and I think we all ought to be interested, in a philosophy projectual rather than descriptive—the latter a qualification that still fits a whole array of theories, from Husserlian phenomenology to Kantian transcendentalism to various versions of empiricism and scientism. The Hegel to which Gadamer and Croce direct us (in whom, as Croce puts it, the history of the spirit does not culminate and terminate in a cusp but unfolds more like a spiral, or, as Gadamer puts it, demands to be halted short of the absolute spirit) is a master of historicity not just as the history of what took place but as authentically the history of what demands to be brought about (a free translation of *Geschichtlichkeit*). There is no historical placing of any author that is not at the same time a utilization of him for the present.

So then: why ought we to be taking up Hegel again now, and not just for historiographical purposes? The answer must start with an overview, taking in neopragmatism in the exemplary version of Richard Rorty, the theory of communicative action, the results of Heideggerian and Gadamerian hermeneutics, and the problems of multiculturalism—in a word, much of what falls under the rubric of the postmodern. In all these phenomena of our culture we encounter what I propose to define as the self-consumption of truth in charity, or as Rorty would call it, in solidarity. It's the same range of things that I tried years ago to encompass in the term "hermeneutic koiné": the fact that in much of contemporary philosophy, including philosophy of science, there is an acknowledgement that truth is not given otherwise than in interpretation. The paradigms of Kuhn, the linguistic games of Wittgenstein, the internal realism of Putnam, and even the communicative action of Habermas (albeit against the Kantian intentions of the author) are all ways of tightly binding the experience of truth to the preliminary aperture of a horizon that works only inasmuch as it is shared. Today I tend to speak more often of truth and charity than of the hermeneutic koiné only because the problems of multiculturalism, which have grown more acute in Western societies in recent decades, require me to render explicit the historical sources of this prevalence of the notion of interpretation. The actuality of hermeneutics and its validity—which I think may still be asserted today—as the common horizon of philosophy and culture is a trait of our historicity linked to the political and social end of Eurocentrism, to the effective transformation of today's industrial societies in a multiethnic and multicultural direction. Neither the truth of the hermeneutic koiné (the prevalence of theories of truth as interpretation) nor the self-consumption of truth in solidarity is an objective description of our situation; they are themselves moments of the coming about of this situation.

How do we respond to the fact (not described from outside but seemingly widely shared as an interpretive perception) of multiculturalism, of the decline of absolute truths, of the relativism that, according to no less an authority than the pope, is spreading everywhere in our daily existence? It appears to me that in neopragmatism we have a summation of the acceptance that truth is given only as the manifestation of a community. What works is what is true. But less and less in the sense of experimental confirmation of a scientific hypothesis; even Popperian falsification doesn't speak of things themselves but only disproves erroneous hypotheses, like an argument *ad homines*. Increasingly, the truth of a statement applies not so much in relation to things themselves (if it ever did) but as a statement that suits or works well for our community, large or small: the local community, the scientific community, our political party, our social class.

Recently I reread Rorty's 1984 essay "Solidarity or Objectivity?" which is one of the most lucid and perspicuous examples of his neopragmatism. An essay like that seems to me the best kind of answer to the question "why Hegel now?" In this essay, Rorty argues his preference for solidarity with reasons that vindicate the validity of relativism, to which solidarity sets bounds that we may, in the end, call objective. I cannot utter whatever pops into my head and claim it as true. But neither can I suppose that I am able to compel assent with apodictic proofs; proofs of that kind will only hold good anyway for those who speak my language, share my background (in mathematics or physics for example), who belong one way or another to a community of which I too am a part. The extreme opposite at which you arrive if you refuse this pragmatist position is the one we see exemplified in the famous résumé of humanity, intended for aliens, that was recently sent into space on a vessel: a few elementary sketches, some mathematical formulas.... The undertaking is not utterly desperate, in the sense that we do hope to find beings like us out there in cosmic space. But if we did find them, understanding would only be made possible by a common culture. Not even a rigorous Kantian could maintain that, by nature, those beings beyond our galaxy would understand a sign as a sign, never mind images or numbers. What we are hoping for when we make a sign or send a message is to encounter someone who understands us because they share a part of our history. The same thing happens in daily communication, in the dialectic between *langue* and *parole*. It happens in aesthetic creation, which Kant sees as aspiring to valid beauty, meaning beauty that is valid in terms of aesthetic judgment, but only on condition of creating, or recreating, a community of taste.

As the reader will see, the territory we are drifting onto is the Hegelian background of neopragmatism and hermeneutic ontology. A statement that "works" always works for someone and in view of some goal. But our fellows who recognize it, or recognize themselves in it, are not pure natural beings; they are made up of hopes, desires, memories. That obviously includes their linguistic competence, which is always marked by the *paroles* incorporated in the *langue* that we and they speak. I might even advance the view that Hegel's thesis that a work of art is a sensible manifestation of the absolute spirit in a certain epoch really boils down to not much more than what I have just formulated in neopragmatist terms. A good reference for this whole line of thought is the long paper delivered by Robert Pippin at the colloquy on "Hegel in America" held in Venice in 2001, to which I owe the initial idea for this text, and many suggestions that I prefer to acknowledge here in blanket fashion rather than spell out (see Pippin 2003). What Pippin, expounding Hegel, says about the State as the realization of liberty appears to me to apply just as well or better to the case of aesthetics. The spirit recognizes itself in institutions inasmuch as the actions that the institutions (the laws) enjoin upon it are felt as its own actions. True, Pippin insists on the view that a citizen may recognize the action as truly his own (as his expression, one might say, using the term in the sense in which Charles Taylor speaks of expressivism à propos of Hegel) when he can justify it and comprehend it as the realization of a rational rule. There is a risk of circularity here, since the rational rule to which I refer to justify the action already presupposes that basic belonging that, in Kant's *Critique of Judgment* and in Hegelian aesthetics, appears rather as the unreflective experience of belonging to a community.

Notwithstanding the differences, I see Pippin as aiming at something analogous to what, inspired by him, I am aiming at here. I mean a form of objectivity very *sui generis*, capable of giving more force to the pragmatist notion of truth as that which works *for us*. Pippin speaks of institutional rationality; I would speak rather of aesthetic rationality or even hermeneutic rationality.

It's a difference that picks up the question of the linkage, in Kant, between the *Critique of Pure Reason* and the *Critique of Judgment*. Although orthodox Kantians may find the proposition audacious, to me it seems clear that the Kantian intellect can function as an organ of objective knowledge of the world, that is, be universally valid, only on the basis of the community that is established, in a manner ever historical and eventual, among the subjects who share the aesthetic experience. Not just in their appreciation of the same works of art or natural beauty but in the acknowledgement of the same civil, religious, and mythical models. . . . This is why even Kant, whatever his intentions, was ethnocentric, and why his philosophy corresponded to a determinate epoch and to its ideal of universalism. Still, no one dreams of calling Kant a relativist on the basis of this irrefutable observation, because, even taking to their extreme the consequences of my thesis, it was still always nature that for him dictated the rules of art through genius. If we leave aside this overly metaphysical doctrine of genius, will we still be able to locate, in the historical community, in the *we* of which Rorty speaks, some sort of guarantee against the arbitrariness of groundless opinion?

Helpful to us here is a philosophical doctrine that indubitably forms part of the moderate reprise of Hegel characteristic of Gadamer: his notion of the "classic." The normativity of the classical models of a culture certainly has a more cogent and objective character than the casual coincidence of tastes or individual opinions uncorroborated by any proof. Yet it is in no sense universally and eternally valid, aspiring to truth in the metaphysical sense of the word. Perhaps, although we are talking about works of art, we could stretch Hegel's own terminology a bit and call it the objective spirit. The classic is what lasts, and in the words of

Heidegger's beloved Hölderlin: "was aber dauert, stiften die Dichter" (that which lasts, poets establish—or found, or create; *stiften* implies all those meanings). It is the notion of the classical, of a historical achievement that becomes a *Wegmark*, a signpost, a reference for entire societies and generations, that endows pragmatic truth, seen as such because it is good *for us*, with authority. It seems to me that only along lines like that could Wittgenstein's linguistic games, or any kind of consensus, even the most scientific, that we might attain in our effort to find the truth be legitimated. Even the classic, when it was founded for the first time by a poet, wasn't yet classical; it corresponded to no preexisting norm, but it wasn't inspired by divine nature either. It was pure eventuation, *Ereignis*, and it only became what it is now by impressing its audience and molding those who esteemed it into a community. The truth of Rortyan neopragmatism is an effect of what Gadamer calls *Wirkungsgeschichte*, the history of the impact something has had. And, to return to Wittgenstein, it is in the concept of the classical that we grasp the closeness of, and also the radical difference between, his analysis of language and Heideggerian hermeneutics.

The latter has a vertical dimension, a historical profundity, that the former lacks. But why must a Heideggerian analysis of language be better than a Wittgensteinian one? To accumulate examples of usage, as we see Heidegger doing in his reconstructions of terms like *veritas*, *aletheia*, or even the verb "to be" itself, which he traces back to Sanskrit, is nothing more than a way of giving the language of today spiritual substance. It is not a foundation that rationally obligates us to accept a certain statement but only a manner of widening its emotive resonance, giving it a cogency that does not in the least imply incontrovertibility. What suits us, what is good for us, is what is woven into the interpretive weave that is history—and not as empty repetition. And it has its own logic inasmuch as it is continuity, *parole* that acquires relief against the background of a *langue* that it thereby modifies and enriches.

Is that all there is to it? The closeness of pragmatist truth to the moderate Hegel of Gadamer has another meaning. The present for the *we* for whom the truth works is always a present that is in motion. Truth is serviceable; there is nothing contemplative about it. Whether or not Hegel really felt himself to be at the end of history, which all the existentialists, starting with Kierkegaard, raised as an objection against him, is doubtful. It is certain that both the reform of dialectic urged by Croce (acutely sensitive to the reasoning of Marx, as we know) and Gadamer's exclusion of the absolute spirit in favor of the objective spirit set the experience of truth within an open horizon of projectuality that strips philosophy of any retrospective character. If there is no absolute to which to return or at which to ultimately arrive, philosophy is caught up in the web of *Wirkungsgeschichte* as a generator of new effects too.

Once again, of course, we need to go beyond a certain superficiality of pragmatism. That which is good *for us*, which reveals itself as that because it corresponds to expectations and needs rooted in our common past, is set free, through the reference to Hegel, from the pure provisionality of a choice entirely contingent and destined to dissolve as the situation changes. What lasts is what the poets found. In recognizing that something is good for us, there is an element of projectuality that aims to become classic, to last, even and especially inasmuch as it strives to hold good for an "us" that is not simply equivalent to the individuals we in fact are. At the horizon line of the near future toward which we gaze, pragmatically assessing the utility of truth, there lies a more distant future that we can never really forget. Rorty alludes to this with the term solidarity, which I propose to read directly in the sense of charity, and not just as the means of achieving consensus but as an end in itself. Christian dogma teaches that *Deus caritas est*, charity is God himself. From a Hegelian viewpoint, we may take this horizon to be that absolute spirit which never allows itself to be entirely set aside but becomes the final horizon of history that legitimates all our nearer-term choices. The absolute character of the spirit consists, for us, not in the fact (as the still somewhat Cartesian Hegel perhaps thinks) of being near to itself in the most total certainty and self-transparency but in constituting the only end toward which all the objective attainments, the pragmatic truths, may aim as the authentic, never totally given, overcoming of every form of alienation.

1. BEYOND THE MYTH OF OBJECTIVE TRUTH

1. For a detailed analysis of the political consequences of the philosophy of Nietzsche and Heidegger, see Vattimo (2003).
2. On the correspondence between hermeneutics and democracy, see Vattimo (2003, chap. 8).
3. For more thorough consideration of Hannah Arendt's politics, see the excellent book by Savarino (1997).
4. The reference is to the statement that "Mussolini never killed anyone," made by the Italian prime minister, Silvio Berlusconi, to the English journalists Boris Johnson and Nicholas Farrell and published in *The Spectator* (September 11, 2003).
5. A slightly modified version of this section was published as chapter 7 of *Nihilism and Emancipation* ("Philosophy, Metaphysics, Democracy"). I have included the essay here because of a necessary theoretical coherence with the theme of this book.
6. On the tendency of much twentieth-century philosophy to take the form of reflection on the contemporary situation, to the point of seeming to be a sort of "sociological impressionism," see Vattimo (1990).

2. THE FUTURE OF RELIGION

1. "Das Sein eigens denken, verlangt, das Sein als den Grund des Seienden fahren zu lassen zugunsten des im Entbergen verborgen spielenden Gebens, d.h. des Es gibt." Martin Heidegger, "Zeit und Sein" (1962), in *Zur Sache des Denkens* (Heidegger 1969). [Vattimo cites this passage from

memory, in the compressed form "Das Sein als Grund fahren lassen," which my translation renders. Compare Joan Stambaugh's translation of the whole sentence in Martin Heidegger, "Time and Being," in *On Time and Being*, trans. Joan Stambaugh (New York: Harper and Row, 1972), 6: "To think Being explicitly requires us to relinquish Being as the ground of beings in favor of the giving which prevails concealed in unconcealment, that is, in favor of the It gives." —WM]

2   I have in mind a survey done several years ago, which led to a book by the Catholic philosopher Pietro Prini, *Lo scisma sommerso* (1999).

3.   This is the title of a great book of fundamental theology by Father R. Garrigou-Lagrange (1914).

3.   THE END OF PHILOSOPHY

1.   A slightly modified version of this section was previously published as chapter 3 in *Nihilism and Emancipation* ("Ethics of Provenance"). I have included the essay because of its necessary theoretical coherence with the theme of this book.

2.   See Plato's *Meno.*

3.   See her translation of Heidegger (1954) in Heidegger, *The End of Philosophy*, trans. Joan Stambaugh (New York: Harper and Row, 1973).

4.   For the meaning of this reprise, see particularly Charles Taylor (1975, 1979).

BIBLIOGRAPHY

The author-date system employed in the text and that heads the entries in this bibliography uses the date of first publication, for obvious historical reasons, but the entries below usually also supply details of more recent and accessible editions. Information (where known) about corresponding English translations follows within the same entry.

Adorno, Theodor W. 1951. *Minima Moralia. Reflexionen aus dem beschadigten Leben*. New ed. Gesammelte Schriften. Frankfurt: Suhrkamp, 1978. *Minima Moralia: Reflections from Damaged Life*. Trans. E. F. N. Jephcott. New York: Schocken, 1978.

Arendt, Hannah. 2002. *Denktagbuch: 1950 bis 1973*. Ed. U. Ludz and I. Nordmann. Munich: Piper.

Auerbach, E. 1946. *Mimesis. Dargestellte Wirklichkeit in der abendländischen Literatur*. Bern: A. Franke. *Mimesis: The Representation of Reality in Western Literature*. Trans. Willard R. Trask, with a new introduction by Edward W. Said. Princeton, N.J.: Princeton University Press, 2003.

Benjamin, Walter. 1940. "On the Concept of History." In Walter Benjamin, *Selected Writings*, Vol. 4, *1938–1940*, trans. Edmund Jephcott et al., 389–400. Cambridge, Mass.: Harvard University Press, 2003. (Original title: "Über den Begriff der Geschichte.")

Bernstein, R. J. 1977. "Why Hegel Now?" *Review of Metaphysics* 31, no. 1: 29–60.

Bloch, Ernst. 1918. *Geist der Utopie*. Faksimile der Ausgabe von 1918. Frankfurt: Suhrkamp Verlag, 1971; Bloch, *Gesamtausgabe*, vol. 16.

Derrida, Jacques. 1967. *De la grammatologie*. Paris: Minuit. *Of Grammatology*. Trans. Gayatri Chakravorty Spivak. Baltimore, Md.: The Johns Hopkins University Press, 1976.

Engel, Pascal, and Richard Rorty. 2005. *À quoi i bon la vérité?* Ed. Patrick Savidan. Paris: Grasset. *What's the Use of Truth?* Trans. William McCuaig. New York: Columbia University Press, 2007.

Fukuyama, Francis. 1992. *The End of History and the Last Man*. New York: Free Press.

Gadamer, Hans-Georg. 1965. "Die philosophischen Grundlagen des zwanzigsten Jahrhunderts." In *Neuere philosophie II*. Tubingen: J. C. B. Mohr, 1987; *Gesammelte Werke*, vol. 4.

Garrigou-Lagrange, R. 1914. *Dieu. Son existence et sa nature*. Paris: Beauchesne.

Habermas, Jürgen. 1992. *Faktizität und Geltung. Beiträge zur Diskursustheorie des Rechts und des demokratischen Rechtsstaats*. Frankfurt: Suhrkamp. *Between Facts and Norms. Contributions to a Discourse Theory of Law and Democracy*. Trans. William Rehg. Cambridge, Mass.: The MIT Press, 1996.

Heidegger, Martin. 1920–1921a. "Anmerkungen zu Karl Jaspers' *Psychologie der Weltanschauungen*." In *Wegmarken*, ed. F.-W. von Herrmann. Frankfurt: Klostermann, 1996; *Gesamtausgabe*, vol. 9. "Comments on Karl Jaspers' Psychology of Worldviews." In *Pathmarks*, ed. William McNeil. New York: Cambridge University Press, 1998.

——. 1920–1921b. *Einleitung in die Phänomenologie der Religion*. In *Phänomenologie des religiösen Lebens*, ed. C. Strube. Frankfurt: Klostermann; *Gesamtausgabe*, vol. 60. *Introduction to the Phenomenology of Religion*, in *The Phenomenology of Religious Life*, trans. Matthias Fritsch and Jennifer Anna Gosetti-Ferencei. Bloomington: Indiana University Press, 2004.

——. 1927. *Sein und Zeit*. Ed. F.-W. von Herrmann. Frankfurt: Klostermann, 1977; *Gesamtausgabe*, vol. 2. *Being and Time*. Trans. Joan Stambaugh. Albany, N.Y.: SUNY Press, 1996.

——. 1935. *Einfuhrung in die Metaphysik*. Frankfurt: Klostermann, 1983; *Gesamtausgabe*, vol. 40. *An Introduction to Metaphysics*. Trans. Gregory Fried and Richard Polt. New Haven, Conn.: Yale University Press, 2000.

——. 1935–1936. "Vom Ursprung des Kunstwerks." In *Holzwege*, ed. F.-W. von Herrmann. Frankfurt: Klostermann, 2003; *Gesamtausgabe*, vol. 5. "The Origin of the Work of Art." In *Off the Beaten Track*, ed. and trans. Julian Young and Kenneth Haynes. New York: Cambridge University Press, 2002.

——. 1946. "Brief über den Humanismus." In *Wegmarken*, ed. F.-W. von Herrmann. Frankfurt: Klostermann, 1996; *Gesamtausgabe*, vol. 9. "Letter on

Humanism." In *Pathmarks*, ed. William McNeil. New York: Cambridge University Press, 1998.

——. 1951. "*Aletheia*." In *Vorträge und Aufsätze*. Neske: Pfullingen, 1954. "*Aletheia* (Heraclitus, Fragment B 16)." In *Early Greek Thinking*, trans. David F. Krell and Frank A. Capuzzi. New York: Harper and Row, 1975.

——. 1954. "Überwindung der Metaphysik." In *Vorträge und Aufsätze*. Neske: Pfullingen, 1954. "Overcoming Metaphysics." In *The End of Philosophy*, trans. Joan Stambaugh. New York: Harper and Row, 1973.

——. 1957. *Identität und Differenz*. Neske: Pfullingen, 1957. *Identity and Difference*. Trans. Joan Stambaugh. New York: Harper and Row, 1969.

——. 1964. "Das Ende der Philosophie und die Aufgabe des Denkens." In *Zur Sache des Denkens*, ed. F.-W. von Herrmann. Frankfurt: Klostermann, 2007; *Gesamtausgabe* vol. 14. "The End of Philosophy and the Task of Thinking." In *On Time and Being*. Trans. Joan Stambaugh. New York: Harper and Row, 1972.

——. 1969. *Zur Sache des Denkens*. Ed. F.-W. von Herrmann. Frankfurt: Klostermann, 2007; *Gesamtausgabe* vol. 14. *On Time and Being*. Trans. Joan Stambaugh. New York: Harper and Row, 1972.

Husserl, Edmund. 1936. *Die Krisis der europäischen Wissenschaften und die transzendentale Phänomenologie*. The Hague: Nijhoff, 1976. *The Crisis of European Sciences and Transcendental Phenomenology*. Trans. David Carr. Evanston, Ill.: Northwestern University Press, 1970.

Kuhn, Thomas S. 1962. *The Structure of Scientific Revolutions*. 3rd ed. Chicago: University of Chicago Press, 1996.

Marconi, Diego. 2007. *Per la verità. Relativismo e filosofia*. Turin: Einaudi.

Nietzsche, Friedrich. 1873. "Über Wahrheit und Lüge im aussermoralischen Sinne." In *Nietzsche Werke. Kritische Gesamtausgabe*, vol. 3.2. Ed. G. Colli, M. Montinari, et al. Berlin: De Gruyter, 1973. "On Truth and Lies in a Nonmoral Sense." In *Philosophy and Truth: Selections from Nietzsche's Notebooks of the Early 1870s*, ed. and trans. Daniel Breazeale. London: Humanities Press International, 1979.

——. 1888. *Götzendämmerung oder Wie man mit dem Hammer philosophiert*. In *Nietzsche Werke. Kritische Gesamtausgabe*, vol. 6.3. Ed. G. Colli, M. Montinari, et al. Berlin: De Gruyter, 1969. *Twilight of the Idols* and *The Antichrist*. Trans. R. J. Hollingdale. Harmondsworth: Penguin, 1968.

Novalis. 1799. "Die Christenheit oder Europa." In *Schriften. Das Philoso-phische Werke* vol. 2.3. Stuttgart: Kohlhammer, 1960. "Christendom or Europe." In *Philosophical Writings,* trans. and ed. Margaret Mahoney Stoljar. Albany, N.Y.: State University of New York Press, 1997.

Pippin, Robert B. 2001. "Hegel on Institutional Rationality." *The Southern Jour-nal of Philosophy* 29 (2001); supplement, "The Contemporary Relevance of Hegel's Philosophy of Right" (2001). "Hegel e la razionalità istituzionale." In *Hegel contemporaneo. La ricezione americana di Hegel a confronto con la tradizione europea,* ed. L. Ruggio and I. Testa. Milan: Guerini, 2003.

Popper, Karl R. 1945. *The Open Society and Its Enemies.* 2 vols. Princeton, N.J.: Princeton University Press, 1971.

Prini, P. 1999. *Lo scisma sommerso.* Milan: Garzanti.

Rorty, Richard. 1984. "Solidarity or Objectivity?" *Nanzan Review of American Studies* 6 (1984); reprinted in *Objectivity, Relativism, and Truth. Philo-sophical Papers, vol. 1.* New York: Cambridge University Press, 1991.

Sartre, Jean-Paul. 1957. *Questions de méthode.* In *Critique de la raison dialec-tique* (1960). *Search for a Method.* Trans. Hazel E. Barnes. New York: Vin-tage, 1968.

——. 1960. *Critique de la raison dialectique précédé de Questions de méthode.* Ed. Arlette Elkaïm-Sartre. 2 vols. Paris: Gallimard, 1985. *Critique of Dialecti-cal Reason, vol. 1, Theory of Practical Ensembles.* Trans. Alan Sheridan-Smith. London: New Left Books, 1976. *Critique of Dialectical Reason,* vol. 2, *The Intelligibility of History.* Trans. Quintin Hoare. London: Verso, 1991.

Savarino, L. 1997. *Politica ed estetica. Saggio su Hannah Arendt.* Turin: Zamorani.

Schürmann, Reiner. 1982. *Le principe d'anarchie. Heidegger et la question de l'agir.* Paris: Seuil. *Heidegger on Being and Acting. From Principles to Anarchy.* Trans. Christine-Marie Gros in collaboration with the author. Bloom-ington: Indiana University Press, 1987.

Taylor, Charles. 1975. *Hegel.* New York: Cambridge University Press.

——. 1979. *Hegel and Modern Society.* New York: Cambridge University Press.

Vattimo, Gianni. 1988. "Ontologia dell'attualità." In *Filosofia '87.* Rome-Bari: Laterza.

——. 1989. *La società trasparente.* Milan: Garzanti. *The Transparent Society.* Trans. David Webb. Baltimore, Md.: The Johns Hopkins University Press, 1992.

——. 1990. "Postmoderno, tecnologia, ontologia." In *Nichilismo ed emancipazione*, ed. Santiago Zabala. Milan: Garzanti. "Postmodernity, technology, ontology." In *Nihilism and Emancipation*, ed. Santiago Zabala, trans. William McCuaig. New York: Columbia University Press, 2004.

——. 2003. *Nichilismo ed emancipazione*. Ed. Santiago Zabala. Milan: Garzanti. *Nihilism and Emancipation*. Ed. Santiago Zabala, trans. William McCuaig. New York: Columbia University Press, 2004.

Wittgenstein, Ludwig. 1921. *Tractatus logico-philosophicus*. Critical ed. by Brian McGuinness and Joachim Schulte. Frankfurt: Suhrkamp, 1989. *Tractatus Logico-Philosophicus*. Trans. D. F. Pears and B. F. McGuinness. New York: Humanities Press, 1961.